Lithofacies, Age, and Sequence Stratigraphy of the Carboniferous Lisburne Group in the Skimo Creek Area, Central Brooks Range

By Julie A. Dumoulin, Michael T. Whalen, and Anita G. Harris

Studies by the U.S. Geological Survey in Alaska, 2006
U.S. Geological Survey Professional Paper 1739–B

Lithofacies, Age, and Sequence Stratigraphy of the Carboniferous Lisburne Group in the Skimo Creek Area, Central Brooks Range

By Julie A. Dumoulin, Michael T. Whalen, and Anita G. Harris

Abstract

The Lisburne Group, a mainly Carboniferous carbonate succession that is widely distributed across northern Alaska, contains notable amounts of oil and gas at Prudhoe Bay. Detailed studies of the Lisburne in the Skimo Creek area, central Brooks Range, delineate its lithofacies, age, conodont biofacies, depositional environments, and sequence stratigraphy and provide new data on its hydrocarbon source-rock and reservoir potential, as well as its thermal history, in this area.

We have studied the Lisburne Group in two thrust sheets of the Endicott Mountains allochthon, herein called the Skimo and Tiglukpuk thrust sheets. The southern, Skimo Creek section, which is >900 m thick, is composed largely of even-bedded to nodular lime mudstone and wackestone intercalated with intervals of thin- to thick-bedded bioclastic packstone and grainstone. Some parts of the section are partially to completely dolomitized and (or) replaced by chert. A distinctive, 30-m-thick zone of black, organic-rich shale, lime mudstone, and phosphorite is exposed 170 m below the top of the Lisburne. The uppermost 40 m of section is also distinctive and made up of dark shale, lime mudstone, spiculite, and glauconitic grainstone. The northern, Tiglukpuk Creek section, which is similar to the Skimo Creek section but only ~760 m thick, includes more packstone and grainstone and less organic-rich shale. Analyses of conodonts and foraminifers indicate that both sections range in age from late Early Mississippian (Osagean) through Early Pennsylvanian (early Morrowan) and document a hiatus of at least 15 m.y. at the contact between the Lisburne and the overlying Siksikpuk Formation. No evidence of subaerial exposure was observed along this contact, which may represent a submarine erosional surface.

Lithofacies and biofacies imply that the Lisburne Group in the study area was deposited mainly in midramp to outer-ramp settings. Deepest water strata are mud rich and formed below storm or fair-weather wave base on the outer ramp to outer midramp; shallowest facies are storm, sand-wave, and shoal deposits of the inner midramp to inner ramp. A relatively diverse, open-marine fauna occurs throughout much of the Lisburne in the study area, but some beds also contain clasts typical of more restricted, shallow-water environments that were likely transported seaward by storms and currents. Radiolarians are abundant in the shale and phosphorite unit at Skimo Creek and also occur in equivalent strata at Tiglukpuk Creek; high gamma-ray response and elevated total organic-carbon contents (max 5–8 weight percent) also characterize this unit at Skimo Creek. Lithologic, faunal, and geochemical data all suggest that these rocks formed mainly in an outer-ramp to basinal setting with low sedimentation rates, high productivity, and poorly oxygenated bottom water. Shale and mudstone at the top of the Lisburne Group accumulated in a similarly sediment starved, mainly outer ramp environment but lack comparable evidence for high nutrient and low oxygen levels during deposition.

Vertical shifts in rock types and faunas delineate numerous parasequences and six probable third-order sequences in the study area; the same sequences are also recognized in the Lisburne Group to the east. Transgressive-system tracts in these sequences generally fine upward, whereas highstand-system tracts coarsen upward. Sequences in the Tiglukpuk Creek section are mostly thinner, contain thinner and more numerous parasequences, and accumulated in somewhat shallower settings than those in the Skimo Creek section. These differences reflect the more seaward position and, thus, increased accommodation space of the Skimo Creek section relative to the Tiglukpuk Creek section during deposition.

Organic-rich calcareous shale in the shale and phosphorite unit has a cumulative thickness of at least 15 m and a lateral extent of >50 km; this lithology is the best potential hydrocarbon source rock in the Lisburne Group at Skimo Creek. The best potential reservoir facies of the Lisburne in the study area is dolomitized crinoidal grainstone that contains intercrystalline, moldic, and vuggy porosity and locally abundant dead oil. Maximum porosities of ~10 percent occur in intervals that are 1 to 2 m thick, of uncertain lateral extent, and best developed near the tops of sequences 1 through 4. Color-alteration indices of conodonts from both the Skimo Creek and Tiglukpuk Creek sections chiefly range from 1.5 to 2, indicating thermal maturities within the oil window.

Introduction

The Lisburne Group consists mainly of Carboniferous carbonate rocks formed within a range of shallow-platform to basinal environments. The Lisburne is discontinuously exposed for >1,000 km in northern Alaska and is widely distributed in the subsurface beneath the North Slope and the Chukchi Sea (fig. 1). It contains an inplace accumulation of ~3 billion bbl of oil and 3 trillion ft^3 of gas in the Lisburne pool at Prudhoe Bay (Jameson, 1994; Dumoulin and Bird, 2001). Deeper-water facies of the Lisburne host phosphate deposits, world-class reserves of zinc and barite, and notable amounts of lead and silver in the central and western Brooks Range (Patton and Matzko, 1959; Moore and others, 1986; Dumoulin and others, 2004; Kelley and Jennings, 2004).

In this chapter, we document the lithofacies, age, and depositional settings of the Lisburne Group in two composite sections in the Skimo Creek area in the central Brooks Range (fig. 2), and propose the first sequence stratigraphic framework for these rocks. We also briefly discuss their thermal history and hydrocarbon source-rock and reservoir potential.

Geologic Setting

The Lisburne Group is essentially undeformed beneath much of the North Slope, but folding and faulting during the Mesozoic and Tertiary Brooks Range orogeny have affected outcrop and subsurface occurrences of the Lisburne to the south and east. In the Brooks Range, the Lisburne is exposed in a series of structural allochthons that are, in turn, made up of smaller thrust plates, sheets, and duplexes (for example, Young, 2004). We measured detailed composite sections of the Lisburne Group in two discrete thrust sheets of the Endicott Mountains allochthon, herein called the Skimo and Tiglukpuk thrust sheets. In both of these sheets, the Lisburne crops out in the core of an anticline; its base is not exposed, and it is overlain by Permian siliciclastic rocks of the Siksikpuk Formation. Regionally, the Lisburne Group overlies Devonian and Mississippian siliciclastic rocks of the Endicott Group. Our sections, on Skimo and Tiglukpuk Creeks (locs. 1 and 2, respectively, fig. 2), are currently ~7 km apart; palinspastic reconstructions suggest that these two sections were originally separated by no more than ~12 to 17 km (R. Swenson, written commun., 2007; W. Wallace, written commun., 2007).

Previous Work, Database, and Methodology

Lithologies and foraminiferal biostratigraphy of the Lisburne Group along Skimo Creek (fig. 2) were reported by Armstrong and others (1970) and Armstrong and Mamet (1977, 1978). Patton and Matzko (1959) and Kurtak and others (1995) described phosphatic rocks in the Lisburne in the study area (fig. 2). Brosgé and Armstrong (1977) presented a generalized section of the upper part of the Lisburne at Tiglukpuk Creek. Geologic maps of the study area include those by Brosgé and others (1960), Kelley (1988, 1990), and Peapples and others (2007). An exploratory petroleum well, Tiglukpuk 1 (fig. 2), was drilled 11 km northeast of our Tiglukpuk Creek section on a Lisburne structural prospect (Oldow and others, 1987); data from this well are still confidential.

We conducted fieldwork in the study area (fig. 2) for 39 days in 2002–5, measuring two composite sections with a Brunton compass and Jacob's staff. The petrographic descriptions presented in this chapter are based on examination of 660 thin sections. Carbonate rocks are classified according to the scheme of Dunham (1962), as modified by Embry and Klovan (1972); when descriptive modifiers are used here, they are listed in order of decreasing abundance. We use the term "supportstone" to encompass packstone and (or) grainstone. Studies of conodonts provide the primary age control for our composite sections; we have integrated these data with previously published ages based chiefly on foraminifers. Our interpretations of depositional settings follow the models of Scholle and others (1983), Burchette and Wright (1992), and Wright and Burchette (1998).

We obtained a gamma-ray profile from the upper part of our Skimo Creek section (fig. 3), using a Scintrex model 512 gamma-ray spectrometer that measures naturally occurring gamma-ray emissions from the rocks. Measurements were taken every 0.5 to 4.0 m, depending on the degree of lithologic heterogeneity. The instrument provides quantitative total gamma-ray and K, U, and Th values. These data yield insight into variations in lithofacies, sedimentary condensation, and sedimentary cyclicity and provide a basis for future correlations of outcrop sections with wireline log data from drill holes on the North Slope (fig. 1).

Lithofacies

Lithofacies of the Lisburne Group in the study area (fig. 2) encompass a range of mainly carbonate rock types. The overall stratigraphic succession of the Lisburne differs somewhat from one thrust sheet of the Endicott Mountains allochthon to another. In this section, we first describe lithofacies of the Skimo Creek section (fig. 3) and correlative rocks in the Skimo thrust sheet and then discuss lithofacies of the Tiglukpuk Creek section (see fig. 9) and coeval strata in the Tiglukpuk thrust sheet to the north.

Skimo Creek Section

The Lisburne Group in the Skimo Creek section (fig. 3) is >900 m thick. Our composite section was measured on the

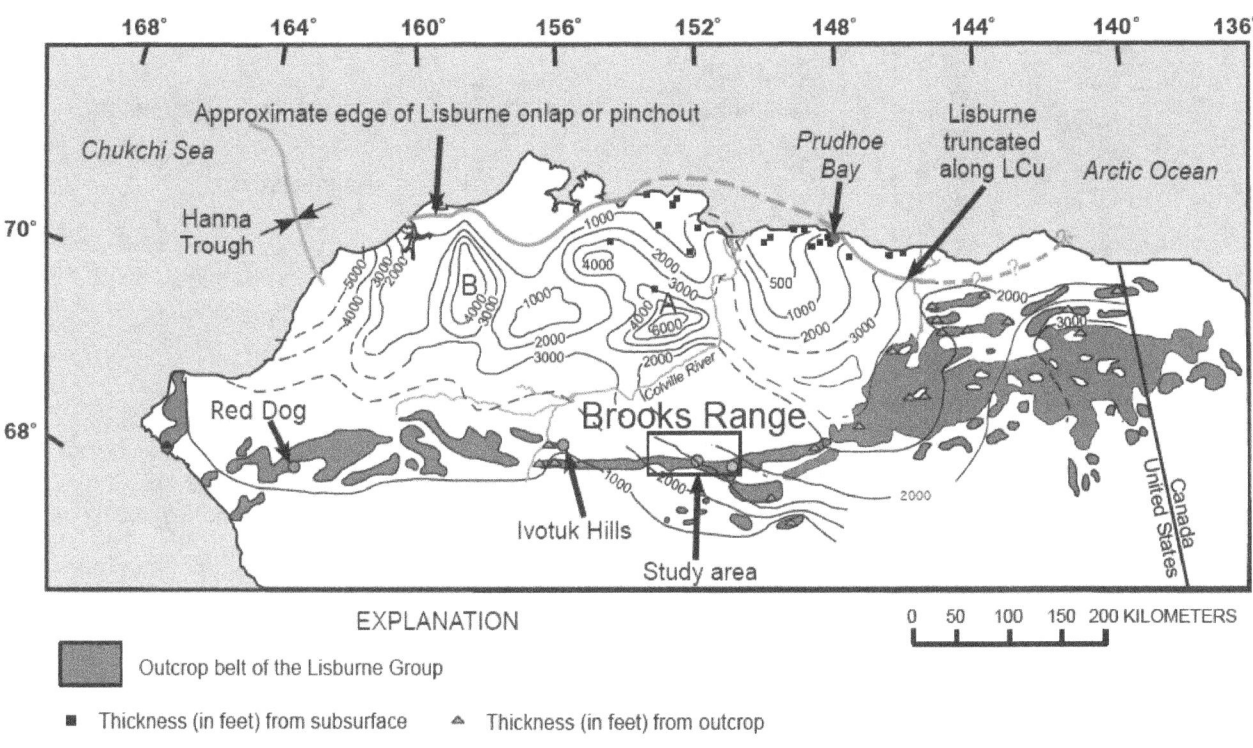

Figure 1. Northern Alaska, showing distribution of the Lisburne Group (after Bird and Jordan, 1977, and Bird, 1988) and locations of study area (see fig. 2) and other places mentioned in text. LCu, Lower Cretaceous unconformity.

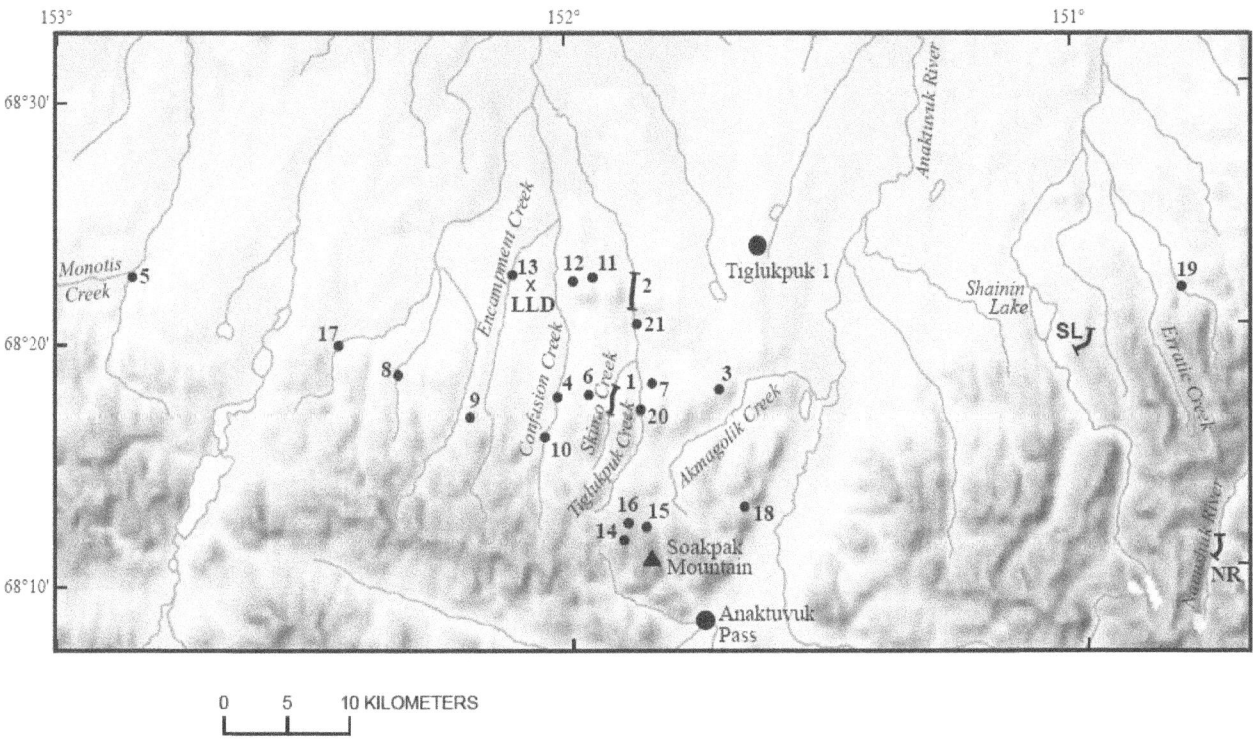

Figure 2. Study area in northern Alaska (fig. 1), showing names and locations of measured sections and lithologic and fossil collections. Numbered dots, localities mentioned in text. LLD, Lawrence Livermore Laboratory drill holes; NR, Nanushuk River section of White and Whalen (2006); SL, Shainin Lake section of Dumoulin and others (1997); Tiglukpuk 1, exploratory well drilled by Chevron.

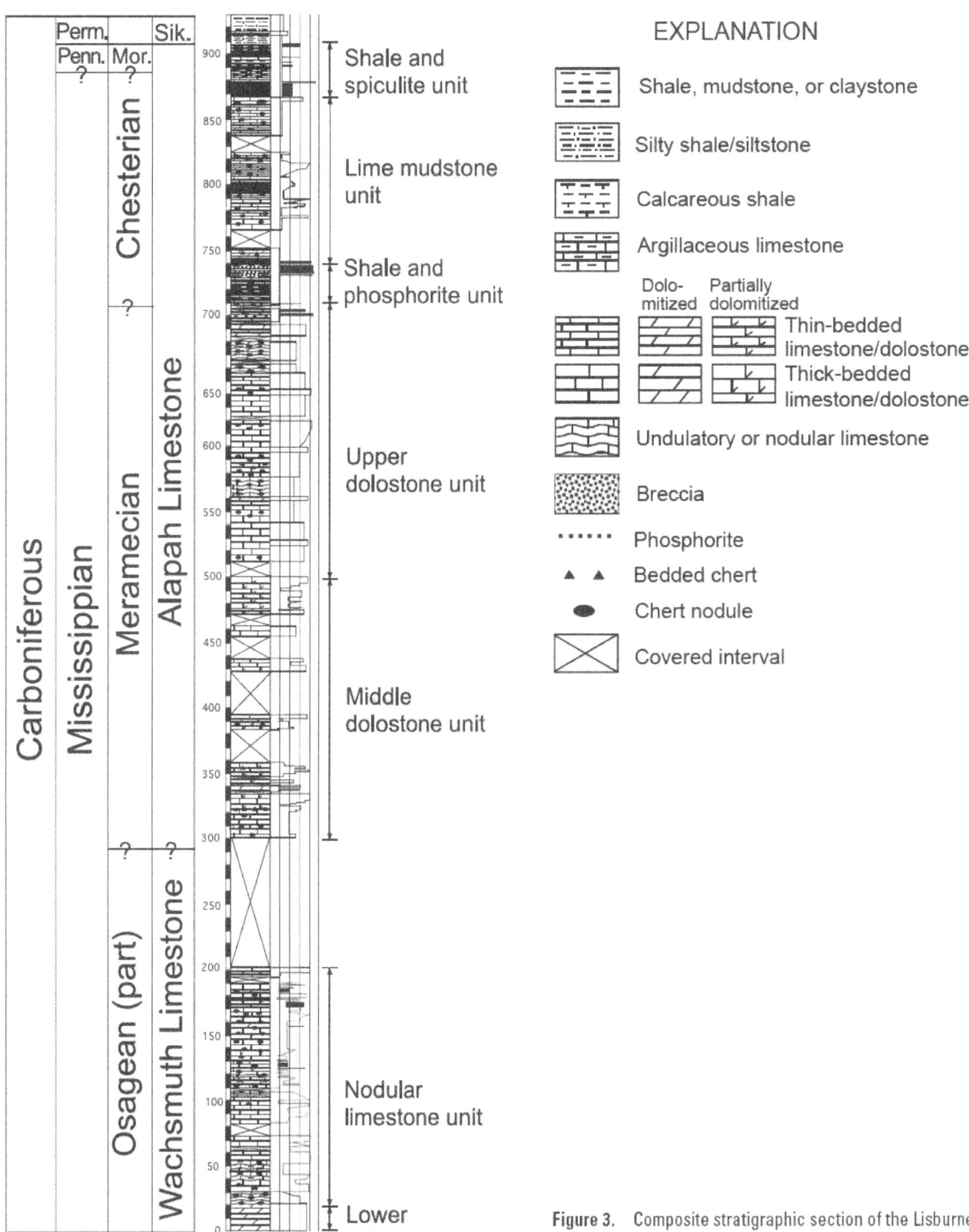

Figure 3. Composite stratigraphic section of the Lisburne Group in the Skimo thrust sheet at Skimo Creek (loc. 1, fig. 2) showing lithologic units discussed in text. Mor., Morrowan; Penn., Pennsylvanian; Perm., Permian; Sik., Siksikpuk Formation. M, mudstone; W, wackestone; P, packstone; G, grainstone; F, floatstone; R, rudstone.

EXPLANATION

Shale, mudstone, or claystone

Silty shale/siltstone

Calcareous shale

Argillaceous limestone

Dolo-mitized   Partially dolomitized

Thin-bedded limestone/dolostone

Thick-bedded limestone/dolostone

Undulatory or nodular limestone

Breccia

Phosphorite

Bedded chert

Chert nodule

Covered interval

north limb of the anticline, mainly along the east side of the creek (loc. 1, fig. 2). The phosphatic rocks in the upper part of the Lisburne are largely covered at stream level; we measured this part of the section along a small ridge just east of, and a few decameters above, the main part of the section. To assess lateral facies variation, we also examined and sampled the upper part of the Lisburne at 10 localities both east and west of the Skimo Creek section, over a distance of ~50 km (fig. 2).

In the central Brooks Range, the Lisburne Group has been divided into the Wachsmuth and overlying Alapah Limestones (Bowsher and Dutro, 1957), the type sections for which are at Shainin Lake, 38 km east of Skimo Creek (fig. 2). Armstrong and Mamet (1977) placed the boundary between these two units at Skimo Creek at ~300 m above the base of the Lisburne, whereas Armstrong and Mamet (1978) designated the boundary at 200 m above this base. A major color change, from darker weathering below to lighter weathering above, is evident about a third of the way up through many Lisburne sections in the central and east-central Brooks Range. We use this color change to mark the top of the Wachsmuth Limestone in the study area (fig. 2), and place it at ~300 m above the base of the Skimo Creek section (fig. 3). A similar contrast in overall weathering color also distinguishes the Wachsmuth from the Alapah Limestone at Shainin Lake.

We recognize a total of seven informal lithologic units in the Lisburne Group at Skimo Creek (loc. 1, fig. 2) on the basis of outcrop features, composition, and weathering characteristics (fig. 3), as well as nine distinct lithofacies that make up these units (table 1): (1) bioclastic grainstone-packstone; (2) nodular mudstone-wackestone; (3) flaggy, argillaceous lime mudstone; (4) wackestone-packstone; (5) calcareous shale and lime mudstone(±chert); (6) phosphatic grainstone-rudstone; (7) lime mudstone; (8) glauconitic siltstone, sandstone, and supportstone; and (9) noncalcareous shale and spiculite. Chert is present but varyingly abundant in most of these units and lithofacies. Most of the chert is light to dark gray, but some is white, brown, or black; it typically forms nodules and bands, a few centimeters to several decimeters thick, but also occurs in irregular zones and patches, some of which appear to represent silicified burrows. Partially silicified intervals are locally common, and bioclasts are preferentially replaced by silica in some beds.

Lower Dolostone Unit

The lower dolostone unit, which makes up the basal 20 m of the main exposure of the Lisburne Group at Skimo Creek (fig. 3), consists of white to medium-gray, pale-yellow-brown- to grayish-brown-weathering dolostone. Beds are mainly 20 to 50 cm thick; 1- to 2-m-thick upward-thickening packages occur in the upper part of the unit. Possible large-scale crossbeds are present locally, and an asymmetric slump, 1.2 m thick and several meters long, cuts the section 14 m above its base (fig. 4B). Thin sections indicate that most of the unit is composed of completely dolomitized crinoidal grainstone and (or) packstone (facies 1B, table 1). Samples from near the base of

the unit have a vuggy porosity of 5 to 10 percent; vugs are as large as 3 mm in diameter, and many are filled or coated with dead oil (fig. 5A). Higher beds contain notable patches of glauconite and phosphate, as well as phosphatic and phosphatized bioclasts that include bryozoans, pelmatozoans, brachiopods, gastropods, and pelecypods.

Beds exposed in a structurally ambiguous position at the center of the Skimo anticline may be partly equivalent to or underlie the base of our main composite section. The beds consist of 8 m of dolostone as described above, overlain by several meters of thin-bedded, undolomitized wackestone-packstone intercalated with thicker bedded, partially to completely dolomitized supportstone (fig. 4A).

Regionally, the Lisburne Group overlies the Kayak Shale, but the contact is not preserved at Skimo Creek (fig. 2). Studies of more complete sections to the east, at Shainin Lake and along the Nanushuk River (fig. 2; Armstrong and Mamet, 1978; Dumoulin and others, 1997; White and Whalen, 2006), suggest that as much as 100 m of the lowermost part of the Lisburne may have been structurally removed in the study area.

Nodular Limestone Unit

The nodular limestone unit, ~180 m thick, overlies the lower dolostone unit (fig. 3). It is distinguished by intervals of nodular cherty limestone, 1 to 10 m thick (figs. 4C, 4D; facies 2, table 1) that occur throughout but are thicker and more abundant in its lower part. Limestone in these intervals is medium to dark gray, weathers brownish gray, forms beds 2 to 30 cm thick, and contains 20–50 percent chert bands and lenses. Most intervals are composed of mudstone and wackestone in the lower part of the unit; wackestone and packstone predominate in the upper part. Two other rock types are intercalated with the nodular limestone: (1) flaggy-bedded, argillaceous lime mudstone that is similar in color but is laminated to thin bedded, contains little or no chert, and forms intervals 0.5 to 2 m thick (facies 3, table 1); and (2) thicker (10–70 cm), even-bedded, medium- to dark-gray lime packstone and grainstone that generally weather light gray, contain ≤25 percent chert, and occur in zones <0.5 to 7.5 m thick (fig. 4D; facies 1A, 1B, table 1).

Bioturbation is common in both mud- and grain-supported rocks throughout the nodular limestone unit, characteristically occurring as millimeter-scale lenses and mottles of muddier limestone within a grainier matrix, or as grainy lenses within a muddy matrix. Grainstones locally contain low-angle crossbeds. Bioclasts are diverse and include pelmatozoan, bryozoan, brachiopod, and possible trilobite fragments, as well as ostracodes, gastropods, foraminifers, algae, and calcispheres (fig. 5B). Solitary and colonial rugose corals occur locally, and calcareous and siliceous sponge spicules are a notable component of nodular limestone in the middle of the unit. Peloids, phosphatic grains, and both phosphatic and phosphatized bioclasts occur in some supportstones in the lower half and uppermost part of the unit; a few of these beds

also contain skeletal grains with micritic rims and possible micritic intraclasts.

Throughout the nodular limestone unit, alternations of mud- and grain-supported rocks define broad packages, ~5 to 30 m thick, as well as smaller scale (max 1–2 m thick) cycles (fig. 4D). In the lower part of the unit, large-scale packages typically consist of even-bedded supportstone, overlain by nodular wackestone and mudstone and (or) flaggy-bedded lime mudstone; in the upper part of the unit, muddier rocks grade upward into packstone and grainstone.

Middle Dolostone Unit

The middle dolostone unit, ~200 m thick, begins ~300 m above the base of the Skimo Creek section and is separated from the underlying nodular limestone unit by a 100-m-thick covered zone (fig. 3). The unit is relatively poorly exposed and includes several covered intervals. Virtually all samples are at least partly dolomitic, and several intervals in the lower half and uppermost part of the unit are completely dolomitized. Exposures are mainly dark gray and weather medium gray to brown-gray, but the most dolomitic strata are light to medium gray on fresh and weathered surfaces. Beds are generally 10 to 50 cm thick. Chert abundance varies but typically is ≤10 percent, although a few zones ~50 m above the base of the unit contain as much as 70 percent irregular chert.

Slightly wavy, parallel laminae are common in the lower half of the middle dolostone unit, and plane laminae occur in some of the highest beds. The bioclast suite is similar to that in the nodular limestone unit; peloids are abundant in some supportstones. Phosphatic and phosphatized skeletal grains are notable in a few wackestone-packstone intervals, mainly in the lower part of the unit. Several of these lower beds contain irregular zones of orange-brown phosphatic(?) chert and (or) phosphatized bioclasts (fig. 5C); the zones may represent firmgrounds or hardgrounds.

Although poor exposure and extensive dolomitization make facies and depositional cycles difficult to discern in the middle dolostone unit, thin sections indicate alternations of mud- and grain-dominated rocks like those visible in the nodular limestone unit. Intervals of nodular and flaggy-bedded lime mudstone and wackestone (facies 2, 3, table 1) occur mainly in the lower 50 m of the unit. Wackestone-packstone and packstone with locally notable parallel laminae (facies 4) occur throughout the unit; these rocks generally contain less mud than facies 2 and 3 but are not as grainy as facies 1. Many of the most dolomitic beds appear to have been packstone and grainstone (facies 1A, 1B) and contain dead oil in intercrystalline and moldic pores and fractures.

Upper Dolostone Unit

The upper dolostone unit, ~200 m thick (fig. 3), resembles the underlying middle dolostone unit in containing several completely dolomitized intervals but is less dolomitic overall, more resistant, and better exposed. Much of the unit forms a narrow gorge along Skimo Creek (fig. 2). Exposures are mainly medium to dark gray and weather pinkish to light brownish gray. Chert abundance varies but is greatest (max 70 percent) near the middle of the unit. Bedding thickness also varies but is notably thick (0.3–1 m) in much of the upper half of the unit. Packstone and grainstone predominate overall and form continuous intervals, ≥20 m thick (facies 1A, 1B, table 1), but are interbedded with subordinate intervals of muddier rocks rich in siliceous spicules (facies 2, 4). Supportstones contain a diverse biotic assemblage like that of the underlying units; a few rocks contain peloids and (or) micritic clasts.

← **Figure 4.** Lithofacies of the Lisburne Group at Skimo Creek (loc. 1, fig. 2). A, Cycles of thin-bedded to nodular wackestone-packstone and thick-bedded dolomitized bioclastic supportstone (facies 1B, table 1), likely formed as sand-wave or shoal deposits in a midramp environment. Strata are probably equivalent to, or directly underlie, lower part of the lower dolostone unit (fig. 3; see text for discussion). B, Irregular, asymmetric lens of dolomitized bioclastic packstone (facies 1B) with abrupt rounded margins, interpreted as a slump structure, near top of the lower dolostone unit (fig. 3). C, Nodular mudstone-wackestone (facies 2) near base of the nodular limestone unit (fig. 3). D, Nodular mudstone-wackestone with argillaceous partings (facies 2) interbedded with bioclastic supportstone (facies 1A) in the nodular limestone unit (fig. 3). Mud-rich strata represent sub-wave-base deposits of outer ramp to midramp; coarser grained beds are likely storm derived. E, Wackestone-packstone with parallel laminae, diverse bioclasts, and 20 to 30 percent black chert (facies 4) in the upper dolostone unit (fig. 3). F, Wackestone-packstone (facies 4) grading to spiculitic wackestone containing as much as 70 percent black chert (facies 2) in the upper dolostone unit (fig. 3). Some chert nodules may replace centimeter-scale burrows. G, Dolomitized peloidal grainstone (facies 1A) at base of the lime mudstone unit (fig. 3) that exhibits straight-crested ripples with a wavelength of 6 to 10 cm and an amplitude of 0.5 to 1 cm, interpreted as wave-worked distal storm deposits on the outer ramp. Ripple crests and troughs are somewhat rounded and relatively symmetrical. H, Flaggy-bedded, argillaceous lime mudstone (facies 3) interbedded with lime mudstone (facies 7) in the lime mudstone unit (fig. 3). Argillaceous intervals are a few centimeters thick or less; lime mudstone interbeds are as much as 10 cm thick. Strata were likely deposited below storm wave base on the outer ramp.

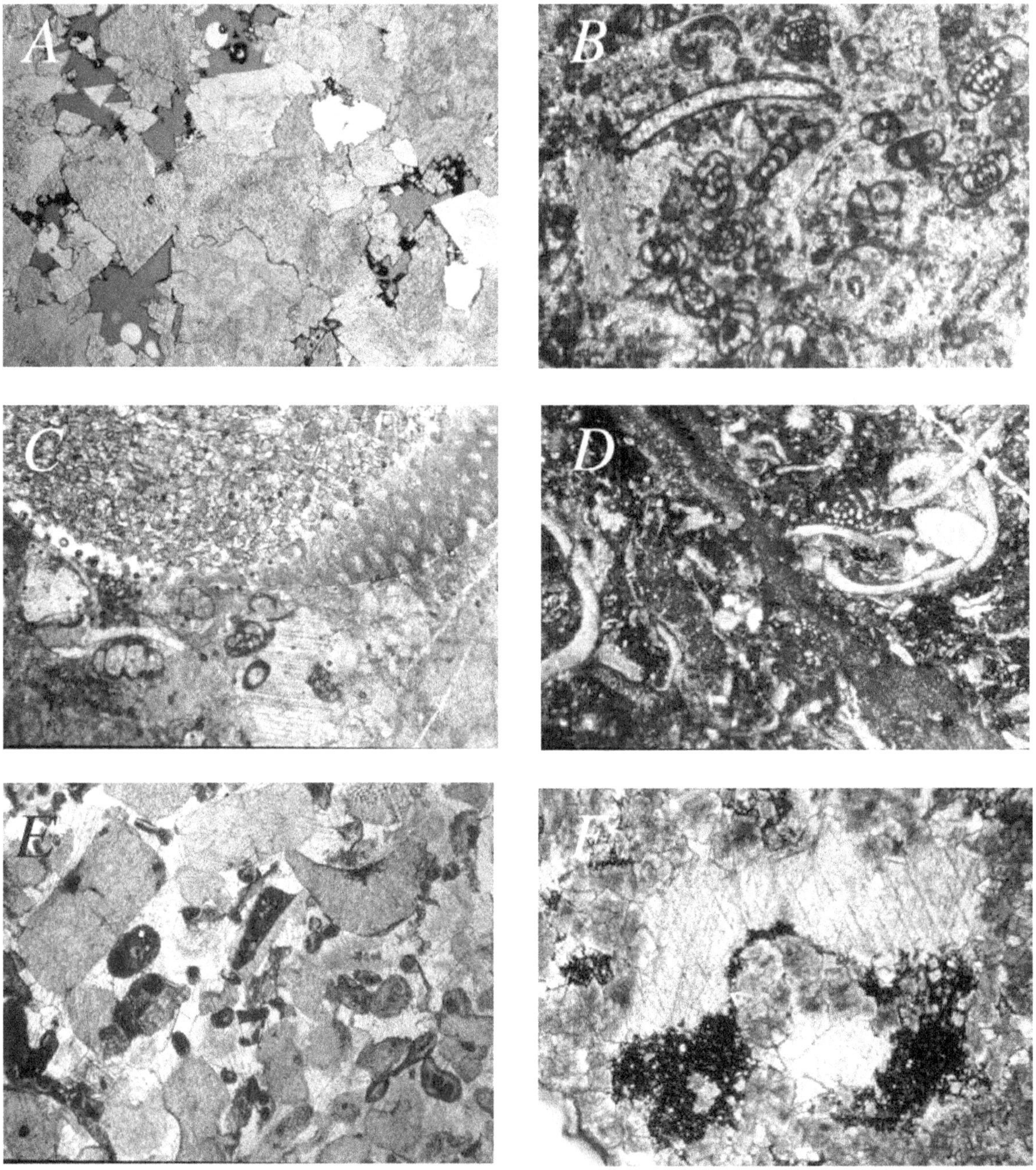

Figure 5.   Photomicrographs of thin sections of samples of the Lisburne Group at Skimo Creek (fig. 2); field of view, 4 mm. *A*, Coarse-crystalline dolostone with relict crinoid fragments, notable intercrystalline porosity (blue areas), and dead oil lining some pores; protolith was likely crinoid grainstone. Facies 1B (table 1), near base of the lower dolostone unit (fig. 3). *B*, Bioclastic packstone-grainstone with abundant foraminifers as well as peloids and algae, interpreted as a storm deposit containing grains carried seaward from inner shelf. Facies 1A, near top of the nodular limestone unit (fig. 3). *C*, Bioclastic packstone-grainstone with crinoid and bryozoan fragments and rare foraminifers. Some bioclasts are phosphatized (note orange-tinted bryozoan fragment in center), and others have thin micritic rims. Deposit may represent a firmground formed during transgression. Facies 1A, lower part of the middle dolostone unit. *D*, Bioclastic wackestone-packstone with ostracodes, subordinate foraminifers, and possible algae. Facies 4, lower part of the middle dolostone unit (fig. 3). *E*, Bioclastic grainstone with open packing; skeletal grains are mainly crinoid and bryozoan fragments. Some bioclasts have thin, discontinuous micritic rims. From thick-bedded interval, >20 m thick, likely deposited in or near shoals of inner midramp to inner ramp. Facies 1B, upper part of the upper dolostone unit (fig. 3). *F*, Coarse-crystalline dolostone with mold after crinoid ossicle filled with dead oil and calcite cement. Facies 1B, near top of the upper dolostone unit (fig. 3).

Table 1.   Lithofacies of the Lisburne Group in the study area.

[See figure 1 for location of study area in northern Alaska. Rock types in parentheses are less common. Cht., chert; dolo., dolostone; G, grainstone; L, lower; lms., limestone; M, mudstone; md., middle; P, packstone; ph., phosphorite; sh., shale; u., upper; W, wackestone]

Facies	Occurrence (Skimo Creek)	Occurrence (Tiglukpuk Creek)	Characteristic features	Interpreted depositional environment
1A Bioclastic packstone-grainstone	Nodular lms. unit Md. dolo. unit U. dolo. unit Lime M unit	Nodular lms.+dolo. unit L. P+G unit Cht.+ph. unit	Intervals <1–2 m thick; beds generally ≤50 cm thick; P, PG, G; bioclasts generally varied, diverse; some intervals have sharp bases and (or) lensoid form; local convolute and plane laminae.	Storm deposits of outer ramp and midramp.
1B Bioclastic packstone-grainstone	L. dolo. unit Nodular lms. unit Md. dolo. unit U. dolo. unit Lime M unit	Nodular lms.+dolo. unit L. P+G unit U. P+G unit	Intervals ≥3–20 m thick; beds generally 20–100 cm thick; P, PG, G; bioclasts generally varied, diverse; commonly crossbedded; locally dolomitized, with vuggy porosity and (or) dead oil.	Sand waves and shoals of midramp and inner ramp.
2 Nodular mudstone-wackestone	Nodular lms. unit Md. dolo. unit U. dolo. unit	Nodular lms.+dolo. unit L. P+G unit ?U. P+G unit	Intervals 1–10 m thick; nodular beds, generally 2–30 cm thick: M, MW, W (WP, P); bioclasts diverse, spicules locally abundant; 20–70 percent chert.	Outer ramp to midramp.
3 Flaggy, argillaceous lime mudstone	Nodular lms. unit Md. dolo. unit Lime M unit	Nodular lms.+dolo. unit L. P+G unit Cht.+ph. unit	Intervals 0.5–2 m (rarely, max 10 m) thick; flaggy to platy beds, generally less than a few millimeters to 10 cm thick: M, MW (W), generally argillaceous; spicules locally abundant; commonly laminated; chert rare to absent.	Outer ramp to midramp.
4 Wackestone-packstone	Md. dolo. unit U. dolo. unit Lime M unit	Nodular lms.+dolo. unit L. P+G unit ?Cht.+ph. unit U. P+G unit	Intervals generally a few meters to several tens of meters thick; even beds, typically 10–40 cm thick; W, WP, P; bioclasts diverse, spicules locally abundant; commonly parallel laminated; generally ≤20, locally ≥50 percent chert.	Midramp.
5 Calcareous shale, lime mudstone (±chert)	Sh.+ph. unit Sh.+spiculite unit	Cht.+ph. unit Sh.+lime M unit	Intervals 7–22 m thick; calcareous shale interbedded with lime mudstone, with shale and limestone sets <0.5–5 m thick; local carbonate concretions (mainly at Skimo Creek) and interbeds of spiculitic chert (mainly at Tiglukpuk Creek): M (MW, W); bioclasts limited to moderately diverse, with locally abundant sponge spicules and radiolarians.	Outer ramp to basin.
6 Phosphatic grainstone-rudstone	Sh.+ph. unit	Cht.+ph. unit	Intervals a few centimeters to 40 cm thick; sand- to pebble-size phosphatic grains in a matrix of calcite, silica, ±fluorite cement and (or) lime or phosphatic mud; phosphatic grains include peloids, ooids, and bioclasts; some beds normally graded, others reversely graded, and some bed bases scoured.	Midramp (to inner ramp?).
7 Lime mudstone	Lime M unit	Absent	Intervals 20–30 m thick; even beds, mainly 2–10 cm thick: M (MW, W); bioclasts limited, with sponge spicules locally abundant.	Outer ramp (to midramp?).
8 Glauconitic siltstone, sandstone, supportstone	Sh.+spiculite unit	Sh.+lime M unit	Intervals a few centimeters to several meters thick; beds 3–30 cm thick; calcareous and (or) quartzose siltstone to sandstone, and (or) bioclastic supportstone with abundant glauconite, phosphatic clasts and bioclasts, and pyrite; abundant burrows, including *Thalassinoides*.	Midramp.
9 Noncalcareous shale and spiculite	Sh.+spiculite unit	Absent	Interval 17.5 m thick; noncalcareous shale with intercalations, 5–150 cm thick, of phosphatic, glauconitic spiculite.	Outer ramp and (or) midramp.

Changes in texture and mud content define several broad cycles in the upper dolostone unit. In the lower third of the unit, grainer rocks give way to muddier ones (figs. 4E, 5D; facies 4, table 1), culminating in a distinctive zone of thin-bedded, nodular cherty spiculitic limestone (fig. 4F; facies 2, table 1). Above this level, three broad cycles, each ~30 to 50 m thick, consist of more chert-rich spiculitic wackestone-packstone (facies 2, 4) overlain by bioclastic packstone and grainstone (fig. 5E; facies 1B, table 1). The highest cycle is largely dolomitized, contains notable parallel laminae, and includes supportstone with vuggy porosity and locally abundant dead oil (fig. 5F).

Shale and Phosphorite Unit

The shale and phosphorite unit, ~30 m thick, consists mainly of calcareous shale and lime mudstone (facies 5, table 1) and various phosphatic strata (figs. 3, 6; facies 6, table 1). Exposures are dark gray to black but generally weather light gray. The shale is organic rich and contains 5 to 8 weight percent total organic carbon (TOC; figs. 6A–6C; see table 5). Phosphatic rock types include phosphatic grainstone to rudstone and nodular/coated-grain phosphorite (figs. 6D, 6E, 7B). Beds consist of sand- to pebble-size phosphatic grains, many with oolitic or oncolitic layering, within a matrix of carbonate and (or) silica cement. Some beds are reversely graded, or contain phosphatic nodules, ≥2 cm in diameter (fig. 6E). Irregular to ellipsoidal concretions of lime mudstone and (or) chert occur locally, ranging from 0.2 to 1 m in maximum dimension.

Calcareous sponge spicules and calcitized and pyritized radiolarians, which are the main bioclasts, are especially notable in lime mudstone in the upper half of the shale and phosphorite unit. Fine details of radiolarian test structure locally are beautifully preserved, particularly in concretions (fig. 7A). Some phosphatic clasts contain radiolarians, sponge spicules, or other skeletal fragments.

Textural and compositional variations within the shale and phosphorite unit indicate the presence of numerous small-scale cycles. The lower 10 m of the unit consists of several thin (10–40 cm thick) beds of lime mudstone that grade upward into intervals of calcareous shale 0.5 to 5 m thick. An irregular layer, a few centimeters thick, of partially silicified skeletal packstone that underlies the lowest mudstone bed appears to represent a lag deposited along a scoured surface. The middle of the unit consists of cycles of shale grading upward into lime mudstone; the cycles thicken upward from <0.5 to 2 m, and the mudstone to shale ratio increases from ≤1:2 to >2:1. The upper part of the unit consists of cycles like those in the middle zone but capped by 5 to 40 cm of phosphatic grainstone to rudstone.

In addition to our detailed sampling at Skimo Creek, we also studied the shale and phosphorite unit ~10 km to the east near Akmagolik Creek, 4.5 km to the west along Confusion Creek, and ~40 km to the west near Monotis Creek (locs. 3–5,

fig. 2). The unit appears to be quite uniform in thickness and overall characteristics throughout this distance. Shale intervals contain as much as 9.4 weight percent TOC at Confusion Creek and 15.0 weight percent TOC at Monotis Creek (see table 5). Phosphatic beds are most abundant at Confusion Creek, where they form at least nine discrete horizons distributed throughout 10 m of section. Goniatite cephalopods were noted at several levels in the Akmagolik Creek section and also observed in the Monotis Creek area, where they had been previously reported by Gordon (1957).

Lime Mudstone Unit

The lime mudstone unit extends for ~130 m from the top of the highest phosphorite bed in the shale and phosphorite unit (fig. 3). Medium- to dark-gray, light-gray-weathering lime mudstone and lesser wackestone predominate (fig. 4H; facies 7, table 1), interbedded with several intervals, ~1.5 to >5 m thick, of similar-colored packstone and (or) grainstone (facies 1A, 1B). Local zones of argillaceous lime mudstone (fig. 4H; facies 3, table 1) and wackestone-packstone (facies 4) also occur in this unit. Beds are generally 2 to 10 cm thick but as much as 30 to 80 cm thick in supportstone intervals; a few muddy zones are finely laminated. Chert abundance is mostly ≤30 percent, but 40–50 percent in parts of the lower half of the unit. Many muddy beds appear to be partly bioturbated. Facies 7 is distinguishable from mud-rich facies 2 and 4 by its less diverse suite of bioclasts (see below), and from facies 3 and 5 by its lower content of argillaceous material and fewer shale interbeds.

The lowest part of the lime mudstone unit is a thin interval of cherty dolostone, whose protolith may have been peloidal grainstone. The base of this interval contains straight-crested ripples, with wavelengths of 6 to 10 cm and amplitudes of 0.5 to 1 cm (fig. 4G). Ripple crests and troughs are somewhat rounded and relatively symmetrical.

Above this basal interval, changes in texture and composition define four cycles, ranging from 15 to 40 m in thickness (fig. 8A). The lowest cycle consists chiefly of mudstone that grades upward into packstone; the three higher cycles are similar but capped with packstone and grainstone. Mudstone throughout the unit generally contains a limited range of bioclasts, mainly sponge spicules and (or) fragments of crinoids, brachiopods, and bryozoans (fig. 7C). Supportstone has a more diverse fauna that includes solitary and colonial rugose corals, ostracodes, foraminifers, and calcispheres, in addition to the bioclast types visible in muddier rocks; peloids, intraclasts, and phosphatic clasts and patches also occur in these strata. Some samples have a fitted fabric with little or no matrix or cement. Bioclast diversity is higher in both muddy and grainy parts of the upper cycles than in texturally equivalent parts of the lower cycles. A thin layer of phosphatic grainstone like that in the shale and phosphorite unit occurs at the top of the lowest cycle. Disarticulated productid brachiopod shells, as much as 10 cm long and oriented both convex side up and convex side down, are abundant on bedding planes in the upper 3 m of the highest cycle.

Figure 6.   Lithofacies of the shale and phosphorite unit (fig. 3) in the Lisburne Group at Skimo Creek
(fig. 2). *A*, Recessive calcareous shale interbedded with more resistant lime mudstone (facies 5, table
1) and phosphatic grainstone and rudstone (facies 6). Unit thickness (and field of view), ~32 m; top of
section is to left. Arrows denote positions and TOC contents (in weight percent) of shale samples (see
table 5). *B*, Cycles of thin-bedded to laminated calcareous shale and mudstone grading upward into
thicker lime mudstone beds (facies 5). *C*, Carbonate concretions in calcareous shale (facies 5). *D*, *E*,
Phosphatic grainstone and rudstone (facies 6). Normally graded phosphatic grainstone with sand-size
peloids, ooids, and bioclasts (fig. 6*D*) is capped by thin rudstone with phosphatic pebbles (fig. 6*E*). These
facies are interpreted as a winnowed, transgressive phosphatized lag and hardground likely deposited
on midramp to inner ramp.

We also studied the uppermost part of the lime mudstone unit at five localities west and east of Skimo Creek (locs. 4, 6–9, fig. 2). In all of these sections, the highest beds in the unit are packstone and grainstone, with a diverse biota that includes foraminifers, algae, and (or) calcispheres. Some skeletal grains in these beds have micritic rims, and others are completely micritized; a few grains appear to have been bored. At two localities, productid brachiopods are concentrated along bedding planes in the highest several meters of section, and rugose corals are abundant in a 2-m-thick zone immediately below. The top of the lowest cycle in the unit at Confusion Creek, as in the Skimo Creek section (fig. 3), contains numerous fine- to coarse-sand-size phosphatic grains.

Shale and Spiculite Unit

The shale and spiculite unit is 40 m thick (fig. 3). Its base is defined by a conspicuous lithologic shift from light-brownish-gray-weathering, resistant supportstone at the top of the underlying lime mudstone unit to relatively recessive black calcareous shale (see fig. 13). Calcareous and noncalcareous shale, spiculite, lime mudstone, and glauconitic grainstone make up the unit, and its top is also marked by a sharp lithologic change from dark-gray, reddish-brown-weathering shale of the uppermost Lisburne Group to bright-yellow-weathering claystone and siltstone of the basal Siksikpuk Formation.

As in the shale and phosphorite unit, compositional and textural variations throughout the shale and spiculite unit define numerous small-scale cycles. The lower half of the unit consists chiefly of interbedded black calcareous shale and dark-gray lime mudstone (fig. 8B; facies 5, table 1). Shale intervals thin upward (from 60 to 1 cm), and mudstone intervals thicken upward (from 15 to 70 cm), through four 1- to 2-m-thick sets in the basal 7 m of section. The shale is fissile and contains 1.7 to 1.8 weight percent TOC (see table 5). The basal limestone is bioturbated mudstone-wackestone with

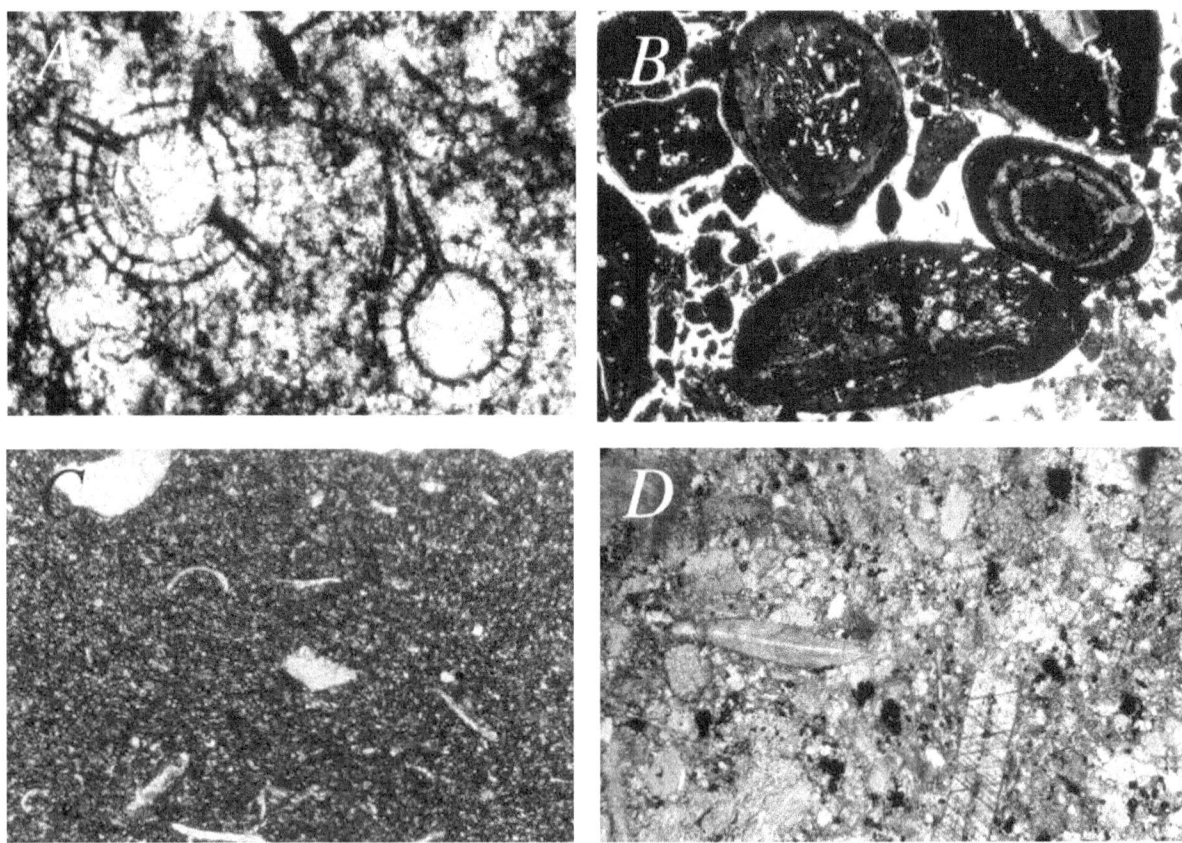

Figure 7.   Photomicrographs of thin sections of samples of the Lisburne Group from the Skimo thrust sheet (*A*) and the Skimo Creek section (*B–D*). *A*, Carbonate concretion with well-preserved radiolarian tests (replaced by pyrite and calcite) within a matrix of fine-grained carbonate. Facies 5 (table 1), upper part of the shale and phosphorite unit at locality 3 (fig. 2). Field of view, 600 μm. *B*, Phosphatic grainstone-rudstone with silica cement; phosphatic clasts include peloids and ooids. Facies 6, upper part of the shale and phosphorite unit (fig. 3). Field of view, 4 mm. *C*, Lime mudstone with rare bioclasts. Facies 7, middle of the lime mudstone unit (fig. 3). Field of view, 4 mm. *D*, Glauconitic, bioclastic grainstone with crinoid and phosphatic skeletal fragments and detrital quartz silt to fine sand. Facies 8, lower part of the shale and spiculite unit (fig. 3). Field of view, 2 mm.

Figure 8. Lithofacies of upper part of the Lisburne Group at Skimo Creek (loc. 1, fig. 2). *A*, Final shallowing-upward cycle within the lime mudstone unit (fig. 3), sequence 5. Cycle is ~40 m thick (arrows); top of section is to right. Beds within cycle thicken and coarsen upward from centimeter-thick lime mudstone (facies 7, table 1), through 10-cm-thick wackestone-packstone (facies 4), to decimeter-thick packstone and grainstone (facies 1B) containing large productid brachiopods and large chert nodules. *B*, Calcareous shale and lime mudstone (facies 5) in lower part of the shale and spiculite unit (fig. 3); thickness of section up to arrow is ~11 m. Arrow denotes location of figures 8*C* through 8*E*. *C*, Thin-bedded to nodular glauconitic siltstone grading upward into glauconitic sandstone and grainstone (facies 8). Beds contain *Thalassinoides*-type burrows filled with glauconitic sandstone and grainstone that penetrate downward from thickest grainstone bed at top. Rectangle denotes location of figure 8*E*. *D*, Upper surface of glauconitic grainstone shown in figure 8*C*. Note green hue due to abundant glauconitic peloids and other grains. *E*, Closeup of glauconitic grainstone at top of succession in figure 8*C*. Note (above pencil) *Thalassinoides*-type burrow filled with glauconitic, phosphatic sandstone. *F*, Interbedded shale and spiculite (facies 9) near top of the shale and spiculite unit (fig. 3); spiculite interval (marked by hammer) forms resistant rib within noncalcareous shale.

minor glauconite and phosphatic pebbles, as large as 1 cm in diameter. Bioclasts in shale and mudstone include bryozoan, crinoid, and brachiopod fragments, ostracodes, foraminifers, sponge spicules, and calcispheres.

At 7 m above the base of the shale and spiculite unit is a distinctive, 45-cm-thick grayish-green interval of 30 cm of glauconitic siltstone to sandstone (grading to supportstone), overlain by 15 cm of coarser grained crinoidal grainstone (figs. 7D, 8C–8E; facies 8, table 1). Productid brachiopods and *Thalassinoides* burrows occur throughout the interval. All rock types contain numerous fine- to coarse-sand-size glauconite clasts, phosphatic clasts and bioclasts, and as much as 10 percent quartz silt and fine sand. Other bioclasts in this interval include ostracode and brachiopod fragments; some skeletal grains have been bored, and some are partly replaced by pyrite.

The glauconitic grainstone is overlain by 17.5 m of calcareous shale interbedded with lime mudstone (facies 5, table 1). Rocks are similar to those in the lower part of the unit, but in the upper half of this interval, shales thicken and lime mudstones thin upward; individual cycles are ~1.5 m thick. The shale contains as much as 1.9 weight percent TOC (see table 5), as well as minor glauconite and quartz silt. Bioclasts are less diverse than in the underlying beds and consist chiefly of brachiopods, ostracodes, and calcareous sponge spicules.

Interbedded shale and spiculite (facies 9, table 1) constitute the upper 15 m of the shale and spiculite unit. The shale is dark gray but weathers reddish brown; it is noncalcareous, locally silty, and forms intervals 1.5 to 6 m thick. The spiculite is medium-dark gray to brownish black, weathers rusty brown, and forms resistant ribs 5 to 150 cm thick (fig. 8F). It consists of a bioturbated mixture of silty lime mudstone, calcareous and siliceous sponge spicules, phosphatic and pyritized bioclasts, glauconite, and as much as 10 percent quartz silt and sand; grainier parts have a wackestone-packstone texture with a matrix of chert, calcite cement, dolomite rhombs, and (or) noncarbonate mud. Higher spiculite beds are coarser grained and contain less mud and more phosphate and glauconite than lower beds. No textural evidence of subaerial exposure was noted in thin section or outcrop at the top of the Lisburne Group.

The shale and spiculite unit is discontinuously exposed along the Brooks Range front in the study area (fig. 2), within the Skimo thrust sheet and an unnamed thrust sheet to the south (Peapples and others, 2007). We examined the unit in this unnamed thrust sheet along Encampment Creek and farther south (locs. 9, 10, fig. 2), as well as to the west within the Skimo thrust sheet (loc. 8, fig. 2). At Encampment Creek, 6 to 9 m of interbedded lime mudstone, calcareous shale, and spiculite overlies 35 cm of glauconitic, phosphatic, crinoidal supportstone that is burrowed, pyritic, and contains bored brachiopod fragments. Spiculitic beds here also include brachiopod fragments, as well as mud-filled burrows. One spiculitic layer at locality 8 contains phosphatic nodules, a few millimeters in diameter, and as much as 30 percent glauconite. Overall lithofacies at these localities are identical to those of correlative strata at Skimo Creek.

Lithofacies much like those of the shale and spiculite unit also occur at the top of the Lisburne Group to the south of the Skimo thrust sheet (Kelley, 1988) near Soakpak Mountain (fig. 2). In that area, however, glauconitic crinoidal grainstone at least locally appears to directly underlie the Siksikpuk Formation (Adams, 1991, 1994).

Tiglukpuk Creek Section

The Lisburne Group is ~725 m thick in the Tiglukpuk Creek section. We measured a continuous section on the south limb of the anticline, as well as a partial section of the lower part of the Lisburne on the north limb; both sections were measured mainly on the east side of the creek (loc. 2, fig. 2). We also examined and sampled some of the upper part of the Lisburne at several localities to the west of our measured section (locs. 11–13, fig. 2). We estimate a thickness of ~760 m for our composite section in the Tiglukpuk thrust sheet and place the top of the Wachsmuth Limestone at ~220 m above the base of this section (fig. 9).

On the basis of composition and bedding style, we have informally subdivided the Lisburne Group on Tiglukpuk Creek (fig. 2) into five units. These units are generally similar to, and correlative with, the units recognized on Skimo Creek but have some notable lithologic differences, described below. Seven of the nine lithofacies recognized at Skimo Creek are also recognized in the Tiglukpuk Creek section (fig. 9).

Nodular Limestone and Dolostone Unit

The nodular limestone and dolostone unit, ~330 m thick (fig. 9), correlates approximately with the lower dolostone, the nodular limestone, and the middle dolostone units at Skimo Creek (fig. 3) and shares some features with all of these units. It contains intervals, generally ≤7 m thick, of nodular limestone (facies 2, table 1) similar in color, composition, and bedding style to those at Skimo Creek, as well as both partially and completely dolomitized zones, although dolomitization appears to be less extensive overall than at Skimo Creek.

Five subunits are recognized in the nodular limestone and dolostone unit on the basis of vertical shifts in carbonate texture and bedding thickness (fig. 9). All the subunits contain some dolomitic limestone; dolostone intervals, 5 and 15 m thick, respectively, occur in the upper two subunits. Subunit 1 (basal 3 m) consists of medium-gray crinoidal grainstone in 30- to 50-cm-thick beds (facies 1B, table 1). The uppermost bed has a closely fitted fabric, contains intergranular dead oil, and has an undulous upper surface with as much as 10 cm of relief; the bed contains abundant and diverse phosphatic and phosphatized bioclasts, including bryozoan and coralline fragments and gastropod steinkerns.

Subunit 2, ~20 m thick, consists mainly of dark-gray to black, thin-bedded, nodular cherty limestone (facies 2, table 1) and platy argillaceous limestone (facies 3). Most samples are wackestones; some platy layers are quite carbonaceous and contain 1 to 2 weight percent TOC (see table 5). Sub-

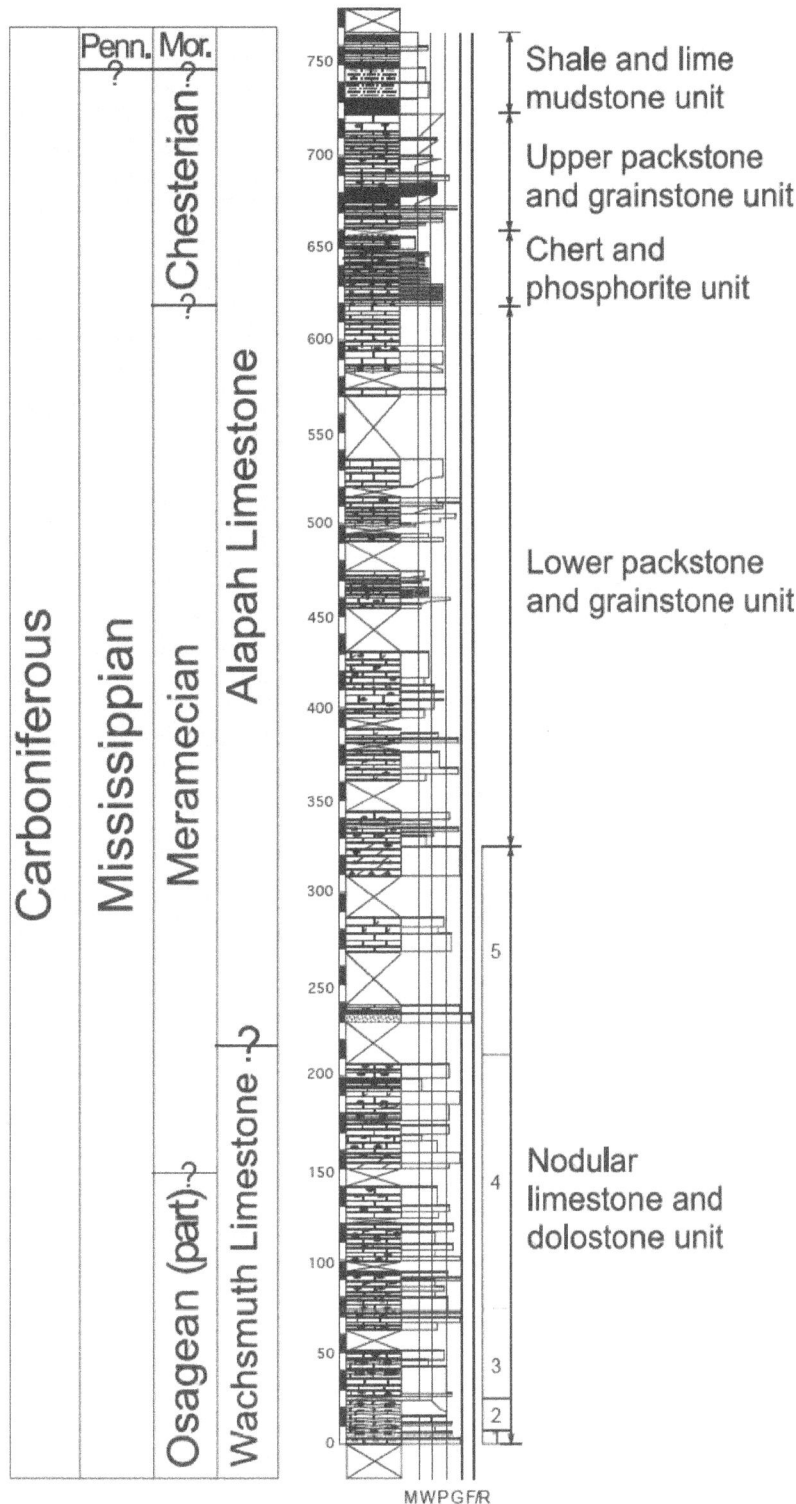

Figure 9. Composite stratigraphic section of the Lisburne Group in the Tiglukpuk thrust sheet, showing lithologic units and subunits 1 through 5 discussed in text. Most of section was measured at locality 2 (fig. 2); upper 35 m was measured at locality 13 (fig. 2). Contact with the overlying Siksikpuk Formation is not exposed in this thrust sheet. Mor., Morrowan; Penn., Pennsylvanian. M, mudstone; W, wackestone; P, packstone; G, grainstone; F, floatstone; R, rudstone. See figure 3 for explanation of symbols.

ordinate intervals, 1 to 2 m thick, of lighter colored, thicker bedded packstone and grainstone (facies 1A) also occur in this subunit. Bioclasts are diverse and include trilobite fragments, rugose corals, siliceous and calcareous sponge spicules, algae, and calcispheres. A few skeletal grains have been bored, and some beds are bioturbated.

Subunit 3, ~50 m thick, is dominantly supportstone. Most beds are medium to dark gray, weather light gray to brownish gray, are 5 to 40 cm thick, and consist of packstone and (or) grainstone (facies 1, mainly 1A, table 1). Thin interbeds and partings of nodular to platy, locally argillaceous wackestone-packstone (facies 2, 3) are organic rich; one sample contained 1.7 weight percent TOC (see table 5). The fauna is similar to that in subunit 2, but lacks siliceous sponge spicules and includes locally abundant foraminifers.

Subunit 4, ~135 m thick, consists of centimeter- to decameter-thick alternations of mud- and grain-supported rocks. It contains intervals of nodular cherty limestone (facies 2, table 1) and platy argillaceous limestone (facies 3) like those in subunit 2, as well as a few beds and partings of calcareous shale. Most limestone intervals are wackestones, and many are rich in siliceous and (or) calcareous sponge spicules; one sample included a fragment of lycopod bark. These muddy strata are intercalated with generally lighter colored, thicker bedded intervals of bioclastic packstone and grainstone, as much as 5 m thick, that contain a diverse biota like that in subunit 3 (facies 1A, 1B). A few samples included subordinate peloids. One supportstone interval is completely dolomitized, has vuggy porosity, and contains notable intercrystalline and vug-filling dead oil; possibly correlative, partially dolomitized grainstone on the north limb of the anticline also contains dead oil. Some grainstone intervals have trough-crossbed sets, as much as 40 to 50 cm thick. Phosphatic and (or) phosphatized bioclasts are locally notable in subunit 4, and several horizons that contain phosphatic(?) chert nodules, irregular burrows, and bored bioclasts may represent firmgrounds or hardgrounds. A distinctive section, at least 10 m thick, of platy argillaceous lime mudstone to wackestone with abundant calcareous sponge spicules and minor quartz silt (facies 3) forms the uppermost part of the subunit.

Much of subunit 5, which comprises the upper 120 m of the nodular limestone and dolostone unit, is covered. Exposures consist mainly of 0.5- to 5-m-thick intervals that grade upward from wackestone (facies 2?, table 1) or wackestone-packstone (facies 4) to packstone and (or) grainstone (facies 1, mainly 1A); these strata contain a diverse fauna like those in the underlying subunits, as well as locally abundant phosphatic and phosphatized bioclasts. A few samples included abundant peloids. Supportstones at the tops of some cycles contain minor glauconite and (or) dead oil. The uppermost 15 m of the subunit is completely dolomitized and locally has vuggy porosity; some pores and fractures are lined with dead oil.

Similarities between the nodular limestone and dolostone unit and correlative strata at Skimo Creek (the lower dolostone through middle dolostone units, fig. 3) are numerous. Significant lithofacies observed in both sections include nodular cherty limestone (facies 2, table 1), argillaceous limestone (facies 3), crossbedded grainstone (facies 1B), and dolomitized supportstone (facies 1B) with local porosity and dead oil. Notable bioturbation, concentrations of phosphatic and phosphatized bioclasts, and cherty, phosphatic(?) horizons that may represent firmgrounds and (or) hardgrounds are other features found at both Tiglukpuk and Skimo Creeks (fig. 2).

Lower Packstone and Grainstone Unit

The lower packstone and grainstone unit, ~290 m thick, correlates with the upper dolostone unit at Skimo Creek (figs. 3, 9). Its base is placed at a sharp lithologic change from light-gray skeletal supportstones to dark-gray chert with subordinate lenses of lime mudstone and wackestone (facies 2?, table 1). The unit is poorly exposed overall, and at least half of it is covered. Alternations of muddier and grainier rocks occur throughout the unit, but supportstones predominate and are especially abundant in the upper 100 m of section. Nodular limestone (facies 2) like that characteristic of the underlying unit is rare and occurs mainly in the lower half of the unit. Minor amounts of platy argillaceous limestone (facies 3) also crop out in this interval. Grain-supported strata (facies 1A, 1B) are generally light to medium gray, weather light gray to light brown, form beds 2 to 100 cm thick, and contain little or no chert; lighter colors and thicker beds characterize grainy rocks in the upper part of the unit. Muddier strata (facies 2–4) range in color from brownish gray to black, are medium bedded to laminated, and typically consist of 30–70 percent chert. Minor to abundant dolomite occurs throughout the unit, particularly in the muddier rocks.

Shifts in bedding thickness, texture, and biota delineate large- and small-scale cycles within the lower packstone and grainstone unit, and the characteristics of these cycles change throughout the unit. The lower half of the unit consists of eight intervals, 5 to 30 m thick, that fine upward; some intervals also display smaller-scale (≤1 m thick) changes in texture. Muddy rocks (facies 2, 4, table 1) dominate the highest intervals. Parallel laminae occur in many of the muddy zones; convolute laminae were noted in a few zones. Both mud- and grain-supported strata are locally bioturbated and contain a diverse biota that includes notable rugose corals and foraminifers. Calcispheres, algae, and peloids were observed mainly in grainier rocks, whereas siliceous and calcareous sponge spicules occurred only in mud-supported strata.

The upper half of the lower packstone and grainstone unit also contains alternations of grainy (facies 1, mostly 1B, table 1) and muddy (facies 4) rocks, but individual cycles, and this interval as a whole, coarsen upward. The bioclast suite in the lower cycles is similar to that in the lower half of the unit but becomes less diverse upward. The upper 35 m of the unit consists mainly of pelmatozoan-bryozoan supportstone that contains few other skeletal grains. Some of these beds are dolomitic, and a few contain minor dead oil. The highest beds are parallel laminated and possibly crosslaminated and include a few grains of glauconite.

General lithofacies of the lower packstone and grainstone unit are similar to those of the upper dolostone unit at Skimo Creek (fig. 2). Both units are partially dolomitized and contain notably thick bedded supportstones in their upper parts. Parallel laminae occur in both units but appear to be more common at Tiglukpuk Creek. The Tiglukpuk Creek section (fig. 9) has more numerous but thinner cycles than equivalent strata at Skimo Creek, and the lower packstone and grainstone unit at Tiglukpuk Creek is less resistant and less well exposed.

Chert and Phosphorite Unit

The chert and phosphorite unit, at least 35 m thick (fig. 9), correlates with the shale and phosphorite unit at Skimo Creek (fig. 3). A sharp lithologic break marks the base of the chert and phosphorite unit; the lowest beds consist of thin-bedded, dark-gray, cherty wackestone-packstone that overlies thick-bedded, light-gray, chert-free grainstone of the underlying lower packstone and grainstone unit.

Several distinctive lithologic packages make up the chert and phosphorite unit. The basal 15 m consists of meter-thick alternations of thicker bedded (max 40 cm), brownish-gray supportstones with local small-scale crossbedding (facies 1A, table 1) and thinner bedded (mostly ≤10 cm thick), dark gray, muddier strata containing 15–60 percent chert (facies 4?). Partial silicification and dolomitization obscure depositional textures throughout the interval, but lime mud and chert increase upward within individual cycles and throughout the interval as a whole. The cherty rocks contain abundant siliceous and lesser calcareous sponge spicules; other bioclasts in this interval include crinoids, brachiopods, bryozoans, ostracodes, and rugose corals. A few phosphatic grains and patches occur near the base of the unit.

The next 10 m of the chert and phosphorite unit consists mainly of thin (2–20 cm thick), partly nodular interbeds of black spiculitic chert, calcareous shale, and argillaceous lime mudstone (facies 5, table 1); parts of this interval are poorly exposed to covered. Bioclastic-peloidal grainstone (facies 1A) containing pelmatozoan fragments, ostracodes, foraminifers, algae, calcispheres, and calcareous sponge spicules occurs near the top of the interval. Some bioclasts in this grainstone have been partially to completely micritized, whereas others have been partially to completely phosphatized. A 4.5-m-thick covered zone above these strata contains a rubble crop of phosphatic grainstone (facies 6) associated with platy lime mudstone (facies 3); these phosphatic rocks are nearly identical to those at Skimo Creek (fig. 3). The highest exposures in the unit are even-bedded to nodular chert and limestone (facies 5), similar to the section below the phosphatic rubble.

Phosphatic grainstone (facies 6, table 1), correlative with that in the Tiglukpuk Creek section (fig. 9), forms rubble and outcrops near the top of the ridge ~3 km to the west (loc. 11, fig. 2). At this locality, a phosphorite bed, 1 to 2 cm thick, is intercalated with dark-gray, brownish-gray-weathering lime mudstone. One thin section from this phosphorite outcrop was composed of four distinct layers, 3 to 10 mm thick, each

with an erosional base and a different matrix composition (including varying proportions of lime and phosphatic mud and calcite and fluorite cement). Phosphatic grains in this thin section included peloids, ooids, and nodules; one layer was reversely graded, and another was normally graded. Other phosphorite samples from this locality had silica cement and numerous phosphatic grains that contained radiolarians and sponge spicules. Associated rock types include black spiculitic chert and brownish-gray skeletal-peloidal grainstone with bored bioclasts and locally abundant brachiopods, as large as 3 cm in diameter.

The chert and phosphorite unit has obvious lithologic similarities to the shale and phosphorite unit at Skimo Creek (fig. 3) but also differs in many respects. Organic-rich shale, which is such a significant component of the shale and phosphorite unit at Skimo Creek, was not observed at Tiglukpuk Creek, although it may underlie parts of the covered intervals. Phosphatic grainstone was observed in only a single horizon at Tiglukpuk Creek, in contrast to Skimo Creek and correlative sections, where it forms at least six discrete layers, although additional phosphatic beds may underlie the covered zones at Tiglukpuk Creek. Chert, generally rich in siliceous sponge spicules, is much more abundant at Tiglukpuk Creek than in the equivalent strata at Skimo Creek, and the Tiglukpuk Creek section includes more grain-supported limestone and less lime mudstone and calcareous shale than do coeval rocks at Skimo Creek. Radiolarians and goniatite cephalopods are locally common at Skimo Creek but rare in the chert and phosphorite unit.

Upper Packstone and Grainstone Unit

The upper packstone and grainstone unit, ~65 m thick (fig. 9), correlates with the lime mudstone unit at Skimo Creek (fig. 3) but is only about half as thick and includes notably less mudstone and more grain-supported strata. The unit is generally similar to the lower packstone and grainstone unit but differs in containing only sparse dolomite.

A covered interval, ~6 m thick, marks the base of the upper packstone and grainstone unit. Cycles of lime mudstone and (or) wackestone-packstone (facies 4, minor facies 2?, table 1) that grade upward into packstone and (or) grainstone (facies 1A, 1B) make up the unit. At least five such broad cycles, each 5 to 15 m thick, were observed, several of which include smaller-scale (≤1 m thick) alternations of muddier and grainier rocks. Mud-supported strata are mostly dark gray, weather brown or tan, and contain 20–50 percent chert; beds are thin (generally 1–15 cm thick) and may be laminated or nodular. Grain-supported strata, in contrast, are typically medium gray, weather grayish brown, and contain little or no chert; beds vary in thickness but commonly are 20 to 100 cm thick. Grainier rocks form parallel-laminated, millimeter- to centimeter-thick lenses in a muddier matrix at several horizons within the unit.

Bioclastic assemblages vary little through the upper packstone and grainstone unit. Pelmatozoan and bryozoan fragments are the dominant skeletal grains; ostracodes, brachiopods, foraminifers, and corals occurred in some samples. Peloids are a subordinate component of support stones in the upper parts of most cycles; other cycle tops contain possible ooids and, near the top of the unit, phosphatic patches and clasts.

The highest beds in the upper packstone and grainstone unit are inaccessible at Tiglukpuk Creek (fig. 2), but we examined them at two localities to the west. About 4.5 km to the west (loc. 12, fig. 2), the upper part of the unit consists of peloidal-skeletal grainstone (facies 1, table 1) containing abundant phosphatic and lime mud peloids, as well as productid brachiopods, gastropods, bryozoan fragments, and phosphatic and phosphatized bioclasts; some bioclasts have been bored, and others have micritic rims. Still farther west, along Encampment Creek (loc. 13, fig. 2), the top of the unit comprises two 1-m-thick beds of light-gray pelmatozoan-bryozoan supportstone, both of which display a notable upward decrease in mud matrix and bryozoan fragments.

Several lithologic differences distinguish the upper packstone and grainstone unit from the coeval lime mudstone unit at Skimo Creek (fig. 3). Supportstone makes up more than half of the upper packstone and grainstone unit but less than 15 percent of the lime mudstone unit. Coarsening-upward cycles are more abundant but thinner at Tiglukpuk Creek (fig. 2). Calcispheres, algae, and completely micritized clasts, present in the upper beds of some cycles at Skimo Creek, were not seen in equivalent strata at Tiglukpuk Creek.

Shale and Lime Mudstone Unit

The uppermost part of the Lisburne Group at Tiglukpuk Creek (fig. 2) is made up of the shale and lime mudstone unit, which is equivalent to the shale and spiculite unit at Skimo Creek. The shale and lime mudstone unit is relatively poorly exposed in the Tiglukpuk Creek section, where it consists of rubble of black, brownish-gray-weathering lime mudstone, wackestone, and calcareous shale in platy to thin (<0.5–3 cm thick) beds (facies 5, table 1). Rare bioclasts include crinoid, brachiopod, bryozoan, and possible trilobite fragments, ostracodes, and phosphatic skeletal grains; chert replaced scattered dolomite rhombs in the lime mud matrix of some samples.

Better exposures of the shale and lime mudstone unit occur ~4.5 km to the west (loc. 12, fig. 2) near the west edge of the Tiglukpuk anticline, ~1 km east of Confusion Creek, where at least 15 m of interbedded lime mudstone and calcareous shale (facies 5, table 1) crops out. The mudstone is dark gray to black, weathers brownish gray to yellowish brown, and forms intervals as much as 30 cm thick made up of 2- to 4-cm-thick beds. Bioclasts are rare and include small brachiopods, ostracodes, crinoid fragments, calcareous spicules, foraminifers, and possible calcitized radiolarians. The shale is black, fissile, and forms layers 10 to 15 cm thick; most samples contain some noncalcareous mud and 5 to 7 percent quartz silt.

The best-exposed and thickest section of the shale and lime mudstone unit examined in this study occurs along the east side of Encampment Creek, ~9 km west of the Tiglukpuk

Creek section (loc. 13, fig. 2), where the unit is ~35 m thick (fig. 9). This section begins with several meters of poorly exposed, bioturbated cherty siltstone made up mostly of quartz silt and siliceous sponge spicules, with 1 to 15 percent glauconite and irregular muddy zones (facies 8, table 1). These beds are overlain by ~5 m of black calcareous shale (facies 5) with several irregular interbeds, 3 to 25 cm thick, of pyritic, glauconitic, quartzose, limy siltstone (facies 8) containing oblique and horizontal trace fossils, gastropods, ostracodes, rugose corals, and phosphatic clasts and bioclasts. The next 15 m of section consists of interbedded lime mudstone and calcareous shale much like that observed near Confusion Creek (facies 5). Mudstone is dominant and forms intervals 0.75 to 1 m thick, with shale interlayers ≤50 cm thick; 5 m of black calcareous shale to shaly lime mudstone constitutes the uppermost beds. Bioturbation is evident throughout the upper 20 m of section, and the bioclast suite in these rocks is like that of coeval strata at Tiglukpuk and Confusion Creeks. One mudstone sample contained notable calcitized radiolarians. The Siksikpuk Formation crops out <100 m south of this locality (Peapples and others, 2007), but its contact with the Lisburne Group here is not exposed.

Lithofacies of the shale and lime mudstone unit are quite similar to those of the correlative shale and spiculite unit at Skimo Creek (fig. 3). Both units consist mainly of limy mud and shale and contain distinctive burrowed, glauconite-rich horizons. Spiculite and noncalcareous shale appear to be less common at Tiglukpuk Creek than in the equivalent beds at Skimo Creek.

Age and Biofacies

Conodonts yield age constraints on the Lisburne Group in the study area (fig. 2) that are in part tighter than those previously published based on foraminifers (Armstrong and others, 1970; Armstrong and Mamet, 1977, 1978) and cephalopods (Gordon, 1957) and also provide data on the biofacies of these rocks. General age ranges of the conodont collections are diagrammed in figures 10 and 11; details of the collections are listed in tables 2 through 4. Correlations of the Mamet foraminiferal zones and American stages used below are those of Poole and Sandberg (1991).

Age

Although the base of the Lisburne Group is not exposed in either the Skimo Creek or Tiglukpuk Creek section, the age of the basal contact is constrained 40 km to the east at Shainin Lake (fig. 2). Here, the underlying Kayak Shale is Kinderhookian (early Early Mississippian), and the lower 280 m of the Lisburne is of probable Osagean age (Dumoulin and others, 1997). Conodonts indicate that the Kayak is also Kinderhookian at locality 16 (fig. 2; table 4), 8.5 km south of the Skimo Creek section (fig. 3).

Conodont and foraminiferal data indicate an Osagean (late Early Mississippian) age for the lower dolostone unit and much, possibly all, of the nodular limestone unit at Skimo Creek (fig. 3). Conodonts demonstrate that the basal 100 m of the Skimo Creek section is no younger than Osagean and no older than middle Kinderhookian (fig. 10; table 2). Foraminifers imply a middle to late Osagean age (Mamet zone 11) for this interval. A conodont collection 180 m above the base (field No. SKIMO 3, table 2) is of tightly constrained latest Osagean-earliest Meramecian age. Foraminifers denote an identical age (Mamet zone 12, Osagean-Meramecian boundary) for this part of the section.

The middle and upper dolostone units are likely of mainly Meramecian (early Late Mississippian) age. Foraminiferal data from the upper two-thirds of the Skimo Creek section (fig. 3) are limited but imply that the lowest part of the middle dolostone unit is definitively Meramecian (Mamet zone 13). Eight conodont collections from these dolostone units yielded mostly sparse faunas consistent with a Meramecian age; overlying collections indicate that these strata are no younger than very earliest Chesterian.

The upper part of the shale and phosphorite unit and the lower part of the lime mudstone unit are tightly dated by conodonts as very early Chesterian (middle Late Mississippian; field Nos. SKBo 20A; SKA 88.3, table 2). This age is compatible with the late Meramecian-early Chesterian age previously interpreted for the shale and phosphorite unit (Dutro, 1987; Dumoulin and others, 1997) on the basis of cephalopods described by Gordon (1957). Conodont collections from the rest of the lime mudstone unit are longer ranging and merely indicate a Chesterian age. Foraminifers from the upper part of this unit also denote a broad Chesterian age (Mamet zones 16–18?). Conodont collections west and south of the Skimo Creek section (locs. 14, 17, fig. 2; table 4) that correlate lithologically and stratigraphically with the top of the lime mudstone unit are also Chesterian, no older than the upper part of the *Gnathodus bilineatus*-Upper *Cavusgnathus* Zone (fig. 10).

Although the lower part of the shale and spiculite unit is definitively Chesterian, the uppermost beds are Pennsylvanian. Conodonts from the glauconitic grainstone 7 m above the base of this unit (field No. SKA 187.1, table 2) are Chesterian (but not very earliest Chesterian) in age. Two collections from spiculite taken just below and at the top of this unit (field Nos. SKA 219, SKA 221, table 2) restrict the age of these beds to early (but not very earliest) Morrowan (Early Pennsylvanian). Yellow-weathering siltstone beds of the basal Siksikpuk Formation that immediately overlie the Lisburne Group here contain Permian foraminifers (Siok, 1985); argillaceous limestone 7 m above the base of the Siksikpuk yielded probable Early Permian conodonts (field No. SKA 230, table 2) and Wolfcampian (early Early Permian) brachiopods (Siok, 1985). These data document a hiatus of at least 15 m.y. (time scale of Gradstein and Ogg, 2004) at the Lisburne/Siksikpuk contact at Skimo Creek.

The Lisburne Group on Tiglukpuk Creek correlates well with the Skimo Creek section (fig. 11; table 3). Crinoidal grainstone at the base of the Tiglukpuk Creek section (base of the nodular limestone and dolostone unit; field No. TNA 1, table 3) is late Kinderhookian-Osagean, and supportstones higher in this unit (field Nos. TNA 43, TNA 94.5, table 3) yielded faunas of Osagean age. Still higher collections within this unit (field Nos. TNB 63, TNB 134.5, table 3) are latest Osagean-earliest Meramecian and correlate precisely with a collection from the Skimo Creek section (field No. SKIMO 3, table 2). Three collections from a partial section in the north limb of the Tiglukpuk anticline (field Nos. TN 1.5, TN 19.3, TN 95.9, table 3) are also contemporaneous. The uppermost part of the nodular limestone and dolostone unit is definitely Meramecian, as is at least part of the lower packstone and grainstone unit (field Nos. TNB 206.2, TNB 264.4, table 3). As at Skimo Creek, the phosphorite interval in the Tiglukpuk thrust sheet is early Chesterian (field No. TNC 197, table 3; loc. 11, fig. 2; table 4). Collections from the upper packstone and grainstone unit also are largely of early Chesterian age. Although the shale and limestone unit was not dated at Tiglukpuk Creek, a sample of glauconitic limestone from near the base of this unit ~9 km to the west (loc. 13, fig. 2; table 4) is early Chesterian.

Collections south and east of Skimo Creek provide additional constraints on the age of the upper part of the Lisburne Group in the study area (fig. 2). Strata near Soakpak Mountain (locs. 15, 18, fig. 2; table 4) are part of an unnamed thrust sheet south of the Skimo thrust sheet; detailed lithofacies of the Lisburne in this sheet are unknown. Skeletal grainstone with abundant phosphatic clasts that occurs at or near the top of the Lisburne northeast of Soakpak Mountain (loc. 18, fig. 2) produced conodonts of latest Chesterian (latest Mississippian) age (field No. SOAK–TOP, fig. 10; table 4). A sample of skeletal wackestone-packstone containing notable glauconite and phosphatic clasts from a similar stratigraphic level but ~8 km to the west (loc. 15, fig. 2; table 4) yielded a latest Chesterian-earliest Morrowan (earliest Pennsylvanian) fauna. East of the Skimo Creek section near Erratic Creek (loc. 19, fig. 2; table 4), crinoidal supportstone with minor glauconite and phosphate ~5 m below the top of the Lisburne produced a fauna of probable very late Mississippian age.

Biofacies

Many conodont collections from the study area (fig. 2) provide information on the depositional setting of the rocks that contain them (tables 2–4). Conodonts from the basal dolostone unit at Skimo Creek (field No. SKIMO 1, table 2) suggest a high-energy, shallow-water setting. Supportstones in the lower and upper parts of the nodular limestone unit (field Nos. SKIMO 2, SKIMO 3, table 2) yielded conodonts of the hindeodid and cavusgnathid biofacies that originated in a shallow-water environment. The higher collection includes *Cavusgnathus hudsoni*, which is typical of warm, shallow-water sequences that may contain evaporites. A collection from this same stratigraphic level but 3 km to the east (loc. 20, fig. 2; table 4) indicates a similar environment.

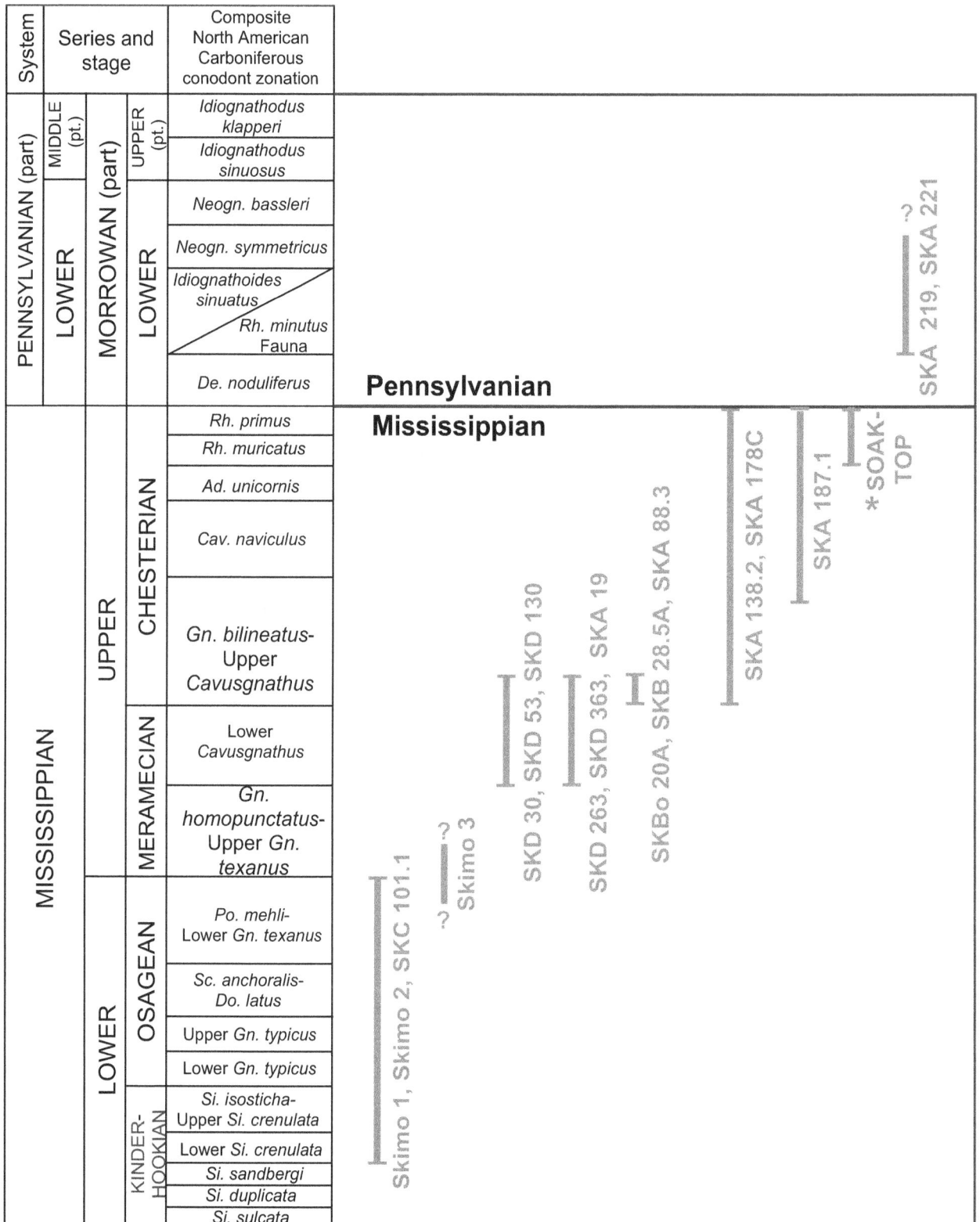

Figure 10. Conodont biostratigraphy of the Lisburne Group at Skimo Creek (fig. 2); see table 2 for details of individual collections. All samples are from Skimo Creek section (loc. 1, fig. 2) except field No. SOAK–TOP, which is from a stratigraphic level likely correlative with field No. SKA 187.1 in a thrust sheet south of the Skimo thrust sheet (loc. 18, fig. 2; table 4). Bars indicate age ranges of individual collections; ages of some collections are constrained by ages of underlying and (or) overlying collections.

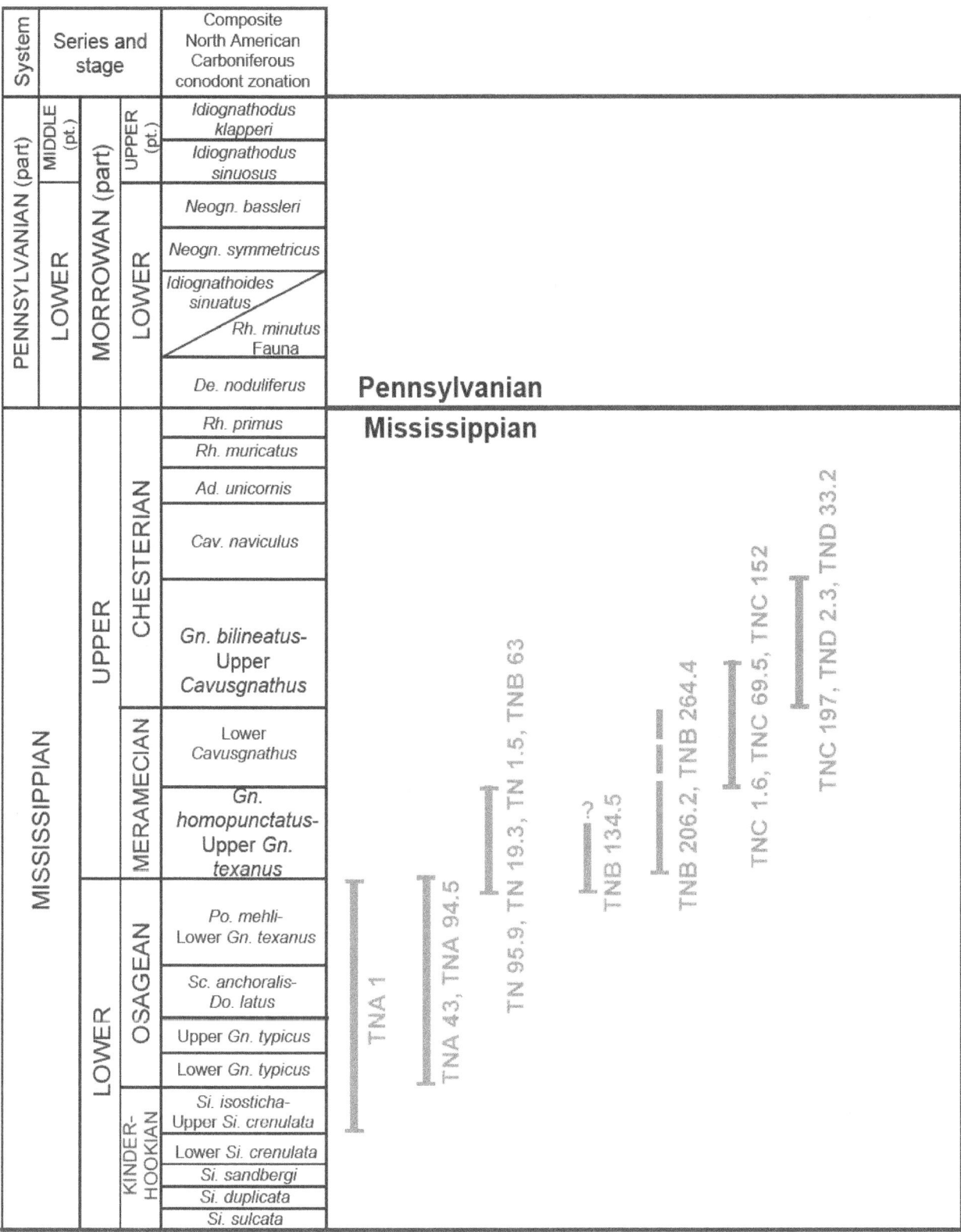

Figure 11. Conodont biostratigraphy of the Lisburne Group at Tiglukpuk Creek (fig. 2). See table 3 for details of individual collections. All samples are from the Tiglukpuk Creek section (loc. 2, fig. 2). Bars indicate age ranges of individual collections; ages of some collections are constrained by ages of underlying and (or) overlying collections.

Conodonts from a packstone interval in the middle dolostone unit (field No. SKD 130, table 2) likely formed as a winnow. Several collections from supportstone in the upper dolostone unit (field Nos. SKD 263, SKD 363, SKA 19, table 2) suggest relatively shallow water depositional settings.

Faunas from carbonate concretions in the shale and phosphorite unit at Skimo Creek (field No. SKBo 20A, table 2) and Monotis Creek (loc. 5, fig. 2; table 4) likely formed as distal winnows into a deep and anoxic depositional environment. Some of the larger specimens in the Monotis Creek fauna may have been deposited by way of fecal pellets.

Conodont assemblages near or at the top of coarsening-upward cycles in the lime mudstone unit (field Nos. SKA 88, SKA138.2, SKA 178C, table 2) represent postmortem transport from shallow-water, locally high-energy (shoal water) settings. Collections from grainstones at the tops of cycles in the lime mudstone unit to the west of Skimo Creek (locs. 4, 8, fig. 2; table 4) were derived from a similar depositional environment, as were assemblages from probably correlative strata farther west (loc. 17) and to the south (loc. 14).

Glauconitic grainstone in the shale and spiculite unit at Skimo Creek (field No. SKA 187.1, table 2) yielded a drowned lag concentrate that represents the relatively deeper water gnathodid biofacies. Strata at or near the top of the Lisburne Group south of the Skimo Creek section (locs. 15, 18, fig. 2; table 4) also produced lag concentrates; these faunas are rich in forms originally deposited in high-energy shoal-water facies.

Biofacies of the Tiglukpuk Creek section (fig. 9) are similar to those at Skimo Creek (fig. 3). Numerous collections from supportstones in the nodular limestone and dolostone unit (field Nos. TNA 1, TNA 43, TNA 94.5, TNB 63, TNB 134.5, TNB 206.2; TN 1.5, TN 19.3, TN 95.9, table 3) indicate postmortem transport from or within relatively shallow water settings. Faunas from the lower packstone and grainstone unit all denote high-energy depositional environments. Conodont assemblages from the chert and phosphorite unit at Tiglukpuk Creek (field No. TNC 197, table 3) and to the west (loc. 11, fig. 2; table 4) are winnows. A fauna collected near the base of the upper packstone and grainstone unit (TND 2.3) indicates postmortem transport from a high-energy environment; a collection from near the top of this unit west of Tiglukpuk Creek (loc. 13, fig. 2, table 4) yielded a mixed biofacies of shallow- and deep-water species.

Depositional Settings

Lithofacies and faunal data suggest that the Lisburne Group in the study area (fig. 2) accumulated chiefly in outer-ramp to midramp settings (table 1). Overall depositional environments in the Skimo Creek and Tiglukpuk Creek sections (figs. 3 and 9, respectively) are quite similar, although some parts of the Skimo Creek section appear to have formed in somewhat deeper water than coeval intervals at Tiglukpuk Creek.

Skimo Creek Section

Lower Dolostone Unit

The lower dolostone unit most likely accumulated in a midramp environment, near but seaward of inner-ramp shoals. Crinoidal supportstone (facies 1B, table 1), the predominate rock type, indicates a relatively high energy depositional environment. Other features of this unit, such as large-scale cross-beds and the scarcity of carbonate mud, support this interpretation, as does the conodont biofacies of collection SKIMO 1 (table 2). Landward shoals may have served as the source for the shallow-water conodonts in this assemblage and could also have provided topographic relief for the generation of slumps like that seen near the top of the unit. The bedding thickness and overall lithology of the lower dolostone unit resemble those of tide- and storm-deposited sand waves and storm lobes documented in the Carboniferous of the Illinois Basin (Lasemi and others, 1998), the Jurassic of Portugal (Azeredo, 1998), and the Cretaceous of Spain (Aurell and others, 1998; Gomez-Perez and others, 1998).

Nodular Limestone Unit

Lithofacies and faunal data indicate a chiefly midramp to outer-ramp setting for the nodular limestone unit. The unit contains some supportstones like those in the lower dolostone unit, but they are intercalated with nodular or flaggy bedded, locally argillaceous lime mudstone and wackestone (facies 2, 3, table 1) that formed in quieter, deeper water below fair-weather wave base. Features of the nodular limestone unit, such as varying bed thickness, nodular beds, abundant carbonate mud, and chiefly normal marine faunas, are typical (for example, Wilson and Jordan, 1983) of midshelf and midramp environments. Deepest water (outer ramp?) settings appear to have prevailed during deposition of the fine-grained, mud- and sponge-spicule-rich limestone intervals in the middle part of the unit. Grain-supported rocks in the nodular limestone unit generally contain some mud and mostly form intervals ≤2 m thick, and thus likely formed as storm deposits (facies 1A, table 1). A few intervals of clean, crossbedded grainstone, 2 to 7 m thick, that occur in the lower and upper parts of the unit may represent near-shoal sand-wave deposits, as described above (facies 1B). Most supportstones contain a diverse, open-marine fauna with a persistent but subordinate component of shallow-water forms, such as foraminifers and algae. These bioclasts, as well as local micritic clasts and peloids, were probably derived from shallower water (inner ramp) settings. Such clasts are especially notable near the top of the unit, as are conodont species characteristic of restricted marine environments (field No. SKIMO 3, table 2; loc. 20, fig. 2; table 4), suggesting that the upper part of the nodular limestone unit formed in a shallowing-upward regime with increasing input from the inner ramp.

Middle Dolostone Unit

Poor exposure complicates interpretation of the depositional environment of the middle dolostone unit, but a mainly midramp setting seems probable. The lower part of the unit contains mud-supported strata like those in the nodular limestone unit (facies 2, 3, table 1), as well as grainier but still mud-rich wackestones and packstones of facies 4. Supportstones (facies 1A, 1B) dominate the upper half of the unit, suggesting a shallowing-upward depositional setting that ranged from the outer to inner midramp. Foraminifers and algae are common in some samples, but a diverse, open-marine biota predominates; peloids are rare. Settings for this unit may have been similar to, but possibly somewhat shallower than, those of the underlying nodular limestone unit because the middle dolostone unit contains less mud and locally more abundant shallow-water faunal elements. Sediment-accumulation rates in the middle dolostone unit may also have been higher because parallel laminae are more common and bioturbation is less evident, implying less time for faunal reworking between depositional episodes.

Upper Dolostone Unit

The upper dolostone unit also likely formed primarily in midramp environments, although variations in lithofacies, bed thickness, and chert abundance indicate some differences in depositional setting. Cherty limestones with abundant siliceous sponge spicules (facies 2, 4, table 1) that accumulated in the deepest water (outer part of the midramp?) are most notable in the middle of the unit. Bioclasts are diverse, but foraminifers and algae are locally significant, and peloids and micritic intraclasts occur in a third of the samples. Three conodont samples from the lower, middle, and uppermost parts of this unit (table 2) all indicate relatively shallow water settings. Supportstones (facies 1A, 1B) dominate the upper dolostone unit, and are thicker bedded (max 1 m), form thicker (≥20 m) continuous intervals, and include more clean grainstones than in the two underlying units. These supportstones are mainly sand-wave and storm deposits of the inner midramp, although some thick-bedded clean grainstones in the upper part of the unit may be inner-ramp shoals.

Shale and Phosphorite Unit

The shale and phosphorite unit records a striking change in the depositional regime of the Lisburne Group at Skimo Creek. The interbedded organic-rich shales and fine-grained carbonate rocks with abundant radiolarians and sponge spicules that make up most of this unit resemble Lisburne facies in the western Brooks Range, such as the Kuna Formation and related rocks (Dumoulin and others, 1993, 2004), and likely formed in a similar environment: an outer-ramp to basinal setting characterized by low sedimentation rates, a nutrient-rich water column, and dysaerobic to anoxic bottom conditions. The lower two-thirds of the unit consists mainly of shale and lime mudstone (facies 5, table 1) deposited below fair-weather (and, possibly, storm) wave base; rare, thin grainy beds probably formed as current lags. Conodont biofacies (tables 2, 4) and a limited, largely pelagic fauna (radiolarians, cephalopods, and sponge spicules) support the interpretation of a deep-water, poorly oxygenated depositional setting. Abundant radiolarians (possibly analogous to modern plankton blooms), high TOC contents (fig. 6A; see table 5), and multiple phosphorite beds suggest high organic productivity, possibly related to upwelling. High TOC contents, as well as strong gamma-ray responses, throughout the unit (see fig. 13) also denote considerable sediment starvation and condensation. Shallower water depths, however, prevailed at times during deposition of the upper part of the unit; phosphorite beds (facies 6) that contain little or no mud were likely deposited above storm wave base and, possibly, close to fair-weather wave base on the midramp. The ooidal layering visible in some phosphatic grains implies considerable wave or current agitation, but at least some of these grains may be carbonate ooids that were carried seaward from inner-ramp settings and subsequently phosphatized. Recognizable bioclasts in phosphatic beds are mainly radiolarians and sponge spicules and include no definitive shallow-water forms.

Lime Mudstone Unit

The lime mudstone unit, which resembles the shale and phosphorite unit in some important ways, likely also accumulated primarily in a deeper water (outer ramp) setting. Mud-rich strata (facies 7, table 1) predominate, as in the underlying unit, but these rocks are thicker and less organic rich than the muddy rocks in the shale and phosphorite unit. The fauna in most of the lime mudstone unit is quite limited (crinoids, brachiopods, bryozoans) but lacks the abundant radiolarians and cephalopods observed in the underlying unit. Phosphatic beds occur locally but are much rarer and generally less phosphatic than in the shale and phosphorite unit. Together, all of these differences suggest that the lime mudstone unit underwent less sediment starvation and condensation and was likely deposited in a better oxygenated, less nutrient rich setting. As in the underlying unit, grain-supported rocks (facies 1A, 1B) cap shallowing-upward cycles. These grainy rocks contain a diverse biota that includes shallow-water forms, such as foraminifers and conodonts, derived from shallow-water, high-energy settings (table 2), as well as peloids and partially to completely micritized grains. Thus, lithofacies and faunal data indicate that although the lime mudstone unit was deposited mainly on the outer ramp, midramp (to inner ramp?) settings were episodically achieved.

Shale and Spiculite Unit

We interpret an outer-ramp to midramp setting for the shale and spiculite unit. Calcareous shale and lime mudstone (facies 5, table 1) that make up most of the lower two-thirds of the unit generally resemble equivalent facies in the shale and phosphorite unit, although the shale in the shale and spiculite unit has notably lower TOC contents and the limestone contains a more diverse fauna that lacks radiolarians and cephalopods but includes rare shallow-water forms, such as foraminifers. An outer-ramp to outer-midramp environment seems likely for these strata—one like that of the shale and phosphorite unit in producing starved, condensed sedimentation but differing in showing no evidence of unusually high productivity or anoxia. The burrowed glauconitic grainstone bed (facies 8), 7 m above the base of the shale and spiculite unit, represents a condensed interval deposited above storm wave base on the midramp; it contains a relatively deep water gnathodid conodont assemblage (table 2). Noncalcareous shale dominates the upper third of the shale and spiculite unit, signaling the end of carbonate input from the Lisburne platform. Coarser grained interlayers in these upper beds are rich in sponge spicules, quartz silt, glauconite, and phosphatic and pyritized clasts and probably formed as current lag deposits. Two such interlayers at the top of the unit yielded conodonts derived from high-energy shoals, supporting interpretation of a shallowing-upward depositional regime. Notable glauconite contents and high gamma-ray responses measured throughout the shale and spiculite unit indicate slow deposition in a sediment-starved setting.

Tiglukpuk Creek Section

Nodular Limestone and Dolostone Unit

Mud- and grain-supported rocks alternately dominate the nodular limestone and dolostone unit, suggesting shifts in depositional regime largely from the outer to inner midramp. Mud-rich strata (facies 2, 3, table 1), which are thickest and most abundant in subunits 2 and 4, likely formed in quiet water below fair-weather wave base. Fine-grained muddy limestone beds rich in siliceous and (or) calcareous sponge spicules that occur mostly near the tops of these subunits were probably deposited in the deepest water (outer midramp) settings. Grain-supported rocks (facies 1A, 1B) make up all of subunit 1 and much of subunits 3 and 5. Most supportstone intervals are <2 m thick, contain a diverse open marine biota, include some mud, and are likely storm deposits. A few thicker (>2 m) zones of clean, crossbedded grainstone and dolomitized grainstone may have accumulated near (or, perhaps, within) inner-ramp shoals. Grains typical of the shallowest water environments, such as foraminifers, algae, and peloids, are a persistent but generally subordinate component of many supportstones and some wackestones throughout this unit; most such grains were probably transported into somewhat deeper water by storms or sand waves. These clasts are especially notable, however, in beds in the middle and upper parts of the unit, where they suggest shallowing-upward conditions. Nine conodont samples from the nodular limestone and dolostone unit, mainly from skeletal grainstones but also from

several packstones (field Nos. TNA 1, TNA 43, TNA 95.5, TNB 63, TNB 134.5, TNB 206, TN 1.5, TN 19.3, TN 95.9, table 3), indicate shallow, or relatively shallow, water; and several collections in subunits 4 and 5 include forms transitional to *Cloghergnathus* sp., a conodont characteristic of environments with elevated salinity (table 3). Lithofacies and faunal data thus suggest that the shallowest water settings (inner midramp, possibly grading to inner ramp) prevailed during deposition of the middle and uppermost parts of the nodular limestone and dolostone unit.

Lower Packstone and Grainstone Unit

The lower packstone and grainstone unit accumulated in midramp to inner-ramp settings. Muddier rocks (facies 2–4, table 1) occur mostly in the lower half of the unit; some of these strata contain abundant sponge spicules. Intercalated supportstones in this part of the unit form relatively thin (<2 m thick) intervals and likely formed as storm deposits (facies 1A), whereas the thick-bedded supportstones that dominate the upper half of the unit probably formed near or within inner-ramp shoals (facies 1B). All the conodont collections from this unit indicate high-energy conditions, and one sample from near the base of the unit includes forms transitional to *Cloghergnathus* sp. possibly derived from an environment with elevated salinity.

Chert and Phosphorite Unit

The chert and phosphorite unit accumulated in a setting much like that in which the shale and phosphorite unit at Skimo Creek (fig. 2) accumulated, but in somewhat shallower water overall. The abundance of mud-rich strata (facies 3, 5, table 1) with a limited biota dominated by siliceous and calcareous sponge spicules indicates a quiet-water, outer-ramp depositional environment for much of the unit. Intervals of crossbedded supportstone (facies 1A) with a more diverse fauna that occur in the lower half of the unit may be contourites and (or) storm deposits derived from midramp sources. Bioclastic-peloidal grainstone (facies 1A) and phosphatic grainstone (facies 6) interbedded with lime mudstone higher up in the unit suggest shallowing-upward cycles. These grainstones contain some constituents typical of very shallow water settings, such as foraminifers, algae, and micritized clasts, implying deposition in an inner-midramp environment with considerable input from even shallower water (inner ramp) sources. Phosphorite beds with locally abundant radiolarians provide evidence of nutrient-rich (upwelling?) conditions like those that prevailed during the deposition of correlative strata at Skimo Creek. Complex textures in some phosphorites, including composite grains and stacked erosional surfaces, denote considerable reworking and condensation in a sediment-starved environment—another similarity to the setting interpreted for the shale and phosphorite unit at Skimo Creek. However, the chert and phosphorite unit at Tiglukpuk Creek (fig. 2) contains more grain-supported strata overall, more sponge spicules (and fewer radiolarians), and more components likely derived from the inner ramp than does the shale and phosphorite unit at Skimo Creek. In addition, organic-rich shale and other indications of an oxygen-starved setting have not been observed at Tiglukpuk Creek. These differences are consistent with a more inboard position for the Tiglukpuk Creek section relative to equivalent strata at Skimo Creek.

Upper Packstone and Grainstone Unit

Lithofacies and faunal data suggest that the upper packstone and grainstone unit accumulated mainly on the midramp. Alternations of muddy strata (facies 2?, 4, table 1) and supportstone (facies 1A, 1B) represent shallowing-upward cycles of quiet-water, sub-wave-base sediment capped by storm and (or) sand-wave deposits. Subordinate peloids and rare foraminifers occur mainly near the tops of these cycles, indicating some input from inner-ramp settings. Conodont biofacies support the interpretation of active storm and (or) current processes that resulted in seaward transport of some faunal elements (field Nos. TND 2.3, TND 33.2, table 3; field No. 05AD9C, table 4).

Shale and Lime Mudstone Unit

The shale and lime mudstone unit, which resembles the lower two-thirds of the shale and spiculite unit at Skimo Creek (fig. 2), likely formed in similar outer-ramp to midramp settings. Most of the unit is mud supported and probably accumulated below fair-weather wave base on the outer shelf to outer midshelf, although spiculitic, glauconitic quartz siltstone intervals were deposited in higher energy (and shallower water?) midshelf settings. Noncalcareous shale interbedded with spiculite forms the uppermost part of the shale and spiculite unit at Skimo Creek but has not been observed in the shale and lime mudstone unit at Tiglukpuk Creek. Similar lithofacies may never have been deposited at Tiglukpuk Creek, or they may be covered—a more likely conjecture because the Lisburne Group-Siksikpuk Formation contact is not exposed in the Tiglukpuk thrust sheet (Peapples and others, 2007).

Sequence Stratigraphy

Sequence stratigraphy divides lithologic successions into chronostratigraphically significant packages bounded by unconformities or correlative conformities (van Wagoner and others, 1988). Our interpretation of the sequence stratigraphy of the Lisburne Group in the study area (fig. 2) is based on documentation of retrogradational, progradational, and aggradational facies-stacking patterns and identification of important stratigraphic surfaces (sequence boundaries, maximum-flooding surfaces, and transgressive surfaces). We recognize six probable third-order sequences (fig. 12), all of which can

be correlated with sequences delineated in the Lisburne to the east (McGee, 2004; White and Whalen, 2006). Whalen and others (2005, 2006) presented preliminary versions of this sequence-stratigraphic framework.

Only transgressive-systems tracts (TSTs) and highstand-systems tracts (HSTs) have been documented in most of our sequences. More detailed analysis might permit the identification of lowstand-systems tracts (LSTs); however, LSTs are difficult to distinguish from HSTs in carbonate ramp successions (Burchette and Wright, 1992). The sequences defined here are thus bounded by transgressive surfaces that are typically indicated by abrupt facies changes from coarser grained, late HST deposits to finer grained, TST deposits. Exact positions of several sequence boundaries are uncertain because of extensive covered intervals (fig. 12).

Sequence 1

As noted above, the base of the Lisburne Group is not exposed in the study area (fig. 2). Sequence 1 is only partly exposed at Skimo Creek and entirely covered at the base of the Tiglukpuk Creek section (fig. 12). At Skimo Creek, sequence 1 consists of the lowermost 20 m of section (lower dolostone unit) that records near-shoal midramp environments. Sequence 1 is fully developed in more complete Lisburne sections to the east in which the contact with the underlying Kayak Shale is preserved. Observations at Shainin Lake (fig. 2; Dumoulin and others, 1997) and in the upper Nanushuk River drainage (fig. 2; Armstrong and Mamet, 1978; White and Whalen, 2006) support the interpretation that the lowest rocks exposed at Skimo Creek record maximum regression, that is, the HST. Correlative shoal and near-shoal facies occur in the Shainin Lake and Nanushuk River sections, where they overlie transgressive deposits of the Kayak Shale and the argillaceous lowermost part of the Wachsmuth Limestone (Dumoulin and others, 1997; Armstrong and Mamet, 1978; White and Whalen, 2006).

Sequence 2

Sequence 2 consists of the nodular limestone unit (~180 m thick) at Skimo Creek and the lower half of the nodular limestone and dolostone unit (~160 m thick) at Tiglukpuk Creek; the exact thickness of this sequence is obscured at both localities by covered intervals (fig. 12). The presence of glauconite and phosphate suggests an abrupt deepening at the top of the lower dolostone unit at Skimo Creek (fig. 3), implying condensed sedimentation during deposition of the TST. The base of the Tiglukpuk Creek section (fig. 9) appears to be above this transgressive surface; thus, the lowermost facies at Tiglukpuk Creek are interpreted to be within the TST. The TST is ~100 m thick at Skimo Creek but only ~20 m thick at Tiglukpuk Creek. In both sections it consists of mud-rich strata with coarser grained supportstone interbeds. We place the maximum-flooding surface within a 20-m-thick package of cherty spiculitic mudstone and

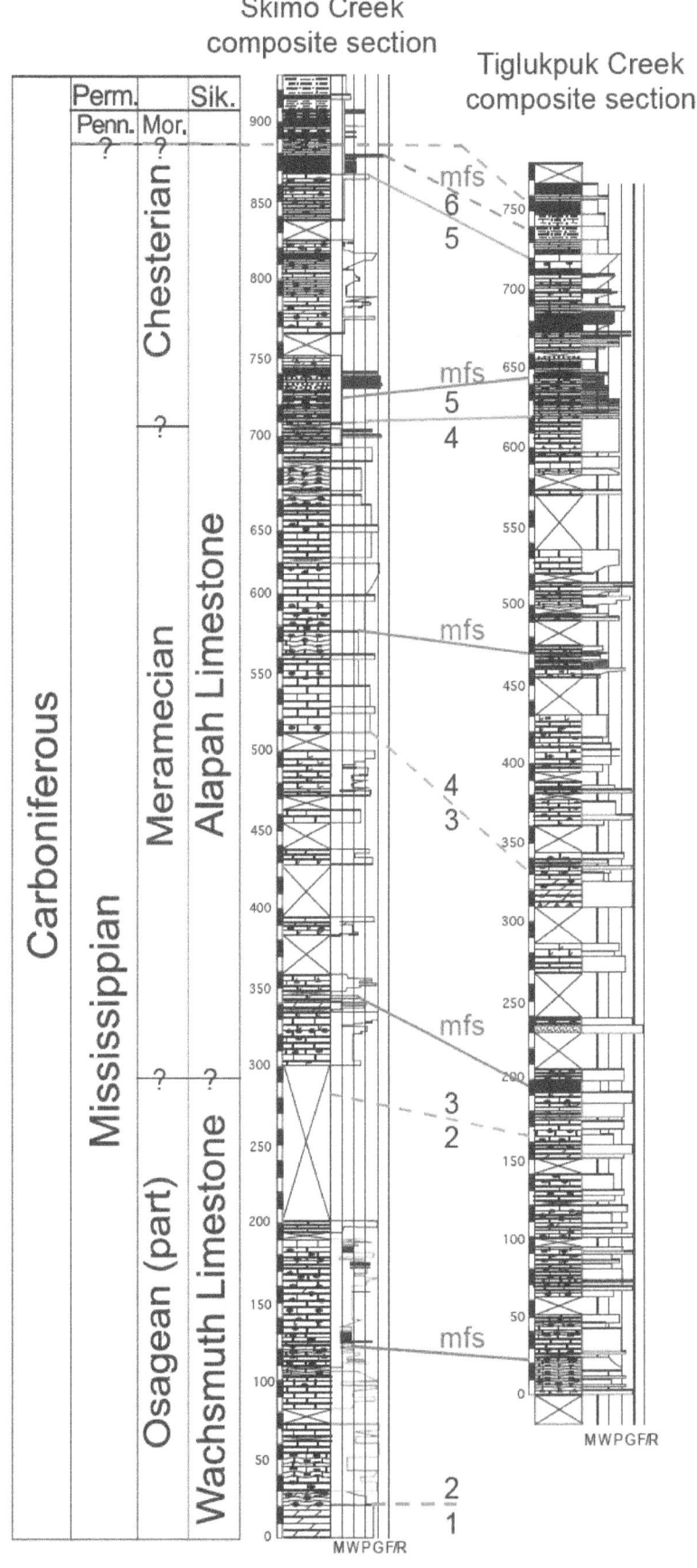

wackestone at Skimo Creek and within an interval of similar lithofacies, at least 5 m thick, at Tiglukpuk Creek. Sooty argillaceous partings within this interval at Tiglukpuk Creek contain 1.77 weight percent TOC, the highest TOC content determined in the Tiglukpuk Creek section. HST deposits at both localities consist of mud-rich strata interbedded with upward-increasing amounts of supportstone, indicating progradation of midramp over outer-ramp or outer-midramp facies. The upper part of this sequence and the sequence boundary likely occur within a 100-m-thick covered zone at Skimo Creek that obscures stratigraphic relations (fig. 12). Poor exposure also complicates recognition of this boundary at Tiglukpuk Creek, but we have tentatively placed it at the top of a 5-m-thick interval of cross-bedded dolomitized grainstone.

Sequence 3

Sequence 3 is ~200 to 250 m thick and includes all of the middle dolostone unit at Skimo Creek (fig. 2); the sequence is slightly thinner (~170 m thick) at Tiglukpuk Creek, where it consists of the upper part of the nodular limestone and dolostone unit (fig. 12). The base and lower part of sequence 3 probably lie within the extensive covered interval at Skimo Creek; mud-supported strata that dominate the next 50 m of exposure are considered part of the TST. Equivalent rocks at Tiglukpuk Creek include more supportstone interbeds but are otherwise similar. Possible firmgrounds or hardgrounds occur at several levels within the TSTs at both localities. We interpret several meters of organic-rich laminated lime mudstone and wackestone to represent maximum flooding at Skimo Creek, and place the maximum-flooding surface at Tiglukpuk Creek within a 10-m-thick interval of platy argillaceous lime mudstone that contains abundant sponge spicules and minor detrital quartz silt; both packages likely formed in outer-midramp settings. Supportstones, which predominate in the upper part of sequence 3 at both localities, represent progradation of progressively shallower midramp environments during the HST.

Sequence 4

Sequence 4 is ~200 m thick and encompasses the upper dolostone unit at Skimo Creek (fig. 2); the sequence is thicker (~290 m thick) and made up of the lower packstone and dolostone unit at Tiglukpuk Creek (fig. 12). The lower boundary of sequence 4 is covered in the Skimo Creek section (fig. 3), but the TSTs at both localities consist of supportstones interbedded with muddier rocks that become more abundant upward. We suggest that maximum flooding at Skimo Creek is represented by 7 m of black, nodular, spiculitic chert and limestone, and at Tiglukpuk Creek by 30 m of partly exposed mud-rich strata containing spiculitic clasts and locally abundant detrital quartz silt. Strata above the maximum-flooding surface at Skimo Creek form three 30- to 50-m-thick cycles (parasequences) that shallow upward from outer-ramp wackestone-packstone to midramp skeletal packstone-grainstone, indicating progradation during deposition of the HST. Overlying the maximum-flooding surface at Tiglukpuk Creek are several thin cycles of platy mudstone or thin-bedded wackestone that grade upward to bioclastic supportstone. Although part of the HST is covered at Tiglukpuk Creek, a thick package of bioclastic supportstone constitutes the uppermost part of sequence 4 here.

Sequence 5

At Skimo Creek (fig. 2), sequence 5 is 160 m thick and consists of the shale and phosphorite and the lime mudstone units; at Tiglukpuk Creek, the sequence is 100 m thick and includes the chert and phosphorite and the upper packstone and grainstone units (fig. 12). The abundance of lime mudstone in the lower part of the sequence at both localities records drowning of the underlying platform during deposition of the TST. At Skimo Creek, thin lime mudstone to shale cycles form the base of sequence 5, indicating deepening upward. We place the maximum-flooding surface at the first spike in the gamma-ray data where TOC contents are highest, coinciding with a shift to shallowing-upward shale to mudstone cycles (fig. 13). Although poor exposure complicates recognition of the maximum-flooding surface at Tiglukpuk Creek, the local presence of phosphatized grains and matrix implies condensation during transgression. We place the maximum-flooding surface at ~640 m in the composite section, where thin calcareous shale is interbedded with spiculitic cherty wackestone-packstone. Overlying cycles at Skimo and Tiglukpuk Creeks grade upward into phosphatic grainstone, likely indicating the earliest highstand deposits. The high gamma-ray response throughout this interval at Skimo Creek (fig. 13) indicates that these facies underwent considerable condensation due to sediment starvation and development of phosphatic hardgrounds. Although the strata deposited during the rest of the HST differ considerably at Skimo and Tiglukpuk Creeks, progradation of midramp supportstones over outer-ramp mudstones occurred at both localities. The cycles at Tiglukpuk Creek, however, are thinner, more numerous, and contain proportionately less mudstone than those at Skimo Creek. The uppermost beds within cycles at both localities contain peloids, grains with micritic rims, and (at Tiglukpuk Creek) rare ooids, indicat-

← **Figure 12.** Sequence stratigraphy of the Lisburne Group at Skimo and Tiglukpuk Creeks (fig. 2), showing sequences 1 through 6 described in text. Red lines, sequence boundaries; blue lines, maximum flooding surfaces (mfs); green line, Mississippian-Pennsylvanian boundary. Lines are dashed where position is equivocal. Parts of sequences below mfs record TST and strata above are HST. Mor., Morrowan; Penn., Pennsylvanian; Perm., Permian; Sik., Siksikpuk Formation. M, mudstone; W, wackestone; P, packstone; G, grainstone; F, floatstone; R, rudstone. See figure 3 for explanation of symbols.

ing shoal or near-shoal environments of the midramp to inner ramp. Sequence 5 marks the final phase of carbonate platform deposition in this part of the central Brooks Range (fig. 1).

Sequence 6

Sequence 6 is ~40 m thick in both the Skimo Creek and Tiglukpuk Creek sections, where it consists of the shale and spiculite unit and the shale and lime mudstone unit, respectively. Previous workers (for example, Kelley and Brosgé, 1995) have called these rocks the "black Lisburne." The dark shales and lime mudstones that overlie the last thick grainstones in sequence 5 indicate an abrupt deepening and drowning of the Lisburne carbonate platform. Four cycles of shale interbedded with lime mudstone that form the lower 7 m of sequence 6 at Skimo Creek (fig. 3) likely constitute most of the TST; glauconitic grainstone with *Thalassinoides* burrows overlies these strata (figs. 8C–8E). Finer grained, burrowed glauconitic siltstone occurs at a similar position in the Tiglukpuk Creek section (fig. 9). Extensive bioturbation, notable glauconite, and (at Skimo Creek) moderately high gamma-ray response (fig. 13) all indicate that these grainy rocks represent significantly condensed intervals (with possible firmgrounds) which could have formed during maximum flooding or as an additional transgressive surface within sequence 6. Interbedded shale and lime mudstone that form the upper part of this sequence in both the Skimo Creek and Tiglukpuk Creek sections could represent highstand deposition or, possibly less likely, continued deepening. In either case, these strata record the final drowning and ultimate demise of the Lisburne carbonate platform.

The nature of the contact between the Lisburne Group and the overlying Siksikpuk Formation remains enigmatic. Fossils document a hiatus of at least 15 m.y. along this boundary. Previous workers (for example, Siok, 1985) considered it a subaerial exposure surface, but we found no textural evidence for subaerial conditions in Lisburne beds directly underlying the Siksikpuk at Skimo Creek (fig. 2). Both the uppermost Lisburne and the basal Siksikpuk at this locality contain faunal elements indicating a fully marine depositional setting: conodonts and sponge spicules in the Lisburne, and foraminifers in the Siksikpuk (Siok, 1985). We suggest that the contact may be a submarine unconformity like those interpreted to occur within Permian carbonate margin successions in the Guadalupe Mountains of Texas by Pray and others (1980) and Franseen and others (1987), who invoked large-scale slumping and bottom-hugging density currents as possible agents of submarine erosion.

Discussion

Lithofacies, age, biofacies, and depositional environments of the Lisburne Group in the Skimo Creek and Tiglukpuk Creek sections (figs. 3 and 9, respectively) are quite similar. Both sections formed primarily in midramp to outer-ramp settings, and both record a significant, penultimate drowning of the Lisburne carbonate platform during the early Chesterian and a second,

final drowning of that platform in the early Morrowan. The first drowning is associated with phosphorite and organic-rich black shale and reflects high productivity, likely linked to upwelling, and dysoxic to anoxic bottom conditions which prevailed at that time throughout much of the Lisburne depositional system in the central and western Brooks Range (fig. 1; Dumoulin and others, 2004). The second drowning is associated with only minor phosphatization and much less organic-rich shale, suggesting that nutrification and low oxygen levels were not significant factors in this event. Tectonically enhanced rates of sea-level rise, due to downdropping of parts of the central Brooks Range along reactivated extensional structures, may have been the principal cause of this second drowning (Whalen and others, 2005, 2006).

Differences between the Lisburne Group in the Skimo Creek and Tiglukpuk Creek sections (figs. 3 and 9, respectively) seem mainly to reflect the more seaward position of Skimo Creek strata during deposition. Generally thinner sequences and thinner, more numerous parasequences at Tiglukpuk Creek may be due to more limited accommodation space farther landward along the ramp. In addition, somewhat deeper water facies than those of coeval intervals at Tiglukpuk Creek occur in parts of the Skimo Creek section. For example, outer-ramp mud-rich facies are more conspicuous in sequences 2, 4, and 5 at Skimo Creek than at Tiglukpuk Creek. Conversely, grainstones that were likely deposited in or near inner-ramp shoals are more common in parts of the Tiglukpuk Creek section than in the Skimo Creek section, particularly in sequence 4.

Hydrocarbon Source Rocks, Reservoir Facies, and Thermal Maturity

In this section, we briefly describe potential hydrocarbon source rocks and reservoir facies of the Lisburne Group in the study area (fig. 2) and summarize available data on the thermal maturity of these sections. Some preliminary results of these studies were reported by Dumoulin and others (2005, 2006b).

Source Rocks

Organic-rich shales of the Lisburne Group in the study area (fig. 2) that are potential hydrocarbon source rocks were first described by Brosgé and others (1981), who reported a TOC content of 5.27 weight percent in a sample collected near locality 7 (fig. 2). Our studies confirm and expand on these findings.

Shale rich enough to be a hydrocarbon source generally contains at least 0.5 weight percent TOC (Tissot and Welte, 1984). Our reconnaissance sampling indicates that Lisburne Group shales with TOC contents above this threshold occur at several stratigraphic levels in both the Skimo Creek and Tiglukpuk Creek sections (figs. 3 and 9, respectively) but are richest and most extensive in the shale and phosphorite unit at Skimo Creek and adjacent localities (locs. 4, 5, 7, fig.

2; table 5). A total of 11 samples of sooty, calcareous black shale from this unit contained 3 to 15 weight percent TOC, and 2 samples of black calcareous phosphorite contained 2 to 3 weight percent TOC. Elevated TOC contents (1.09–1.88 weight percent) were also measured in calcareous shale and argillaceous limestone in the nodular limestone and dolostone unit at Tiglukpuk Creek and in calcareous black shale in the shale and spiculite unit at Skimo Creek.

On the basis of both TOC contents and lithofacies-distribution data, the shale and phosphorite unit appears to be an excellent potential hydrocarbon source rock. Organic-rich shale makes up at least half of this unit and has a cumulative thickness of more than 15 m. All the shale samples from the unit have high TOC contents (mostly ≥5 weight percent, table 5). The shale and phosphorite unit extends for >50 km throughout the west half of the Chandler Lake quadrangle (Kelley, 1988; Peapples and others, 2007) and was penetrated in the subsurface (Brosgé and Armstrong, 1977) in two shallow test holes drilled by the Lawrence Livermore Laboratory west of Confusion Creek (loc. LLD, fig. 2). Equivalent rocks

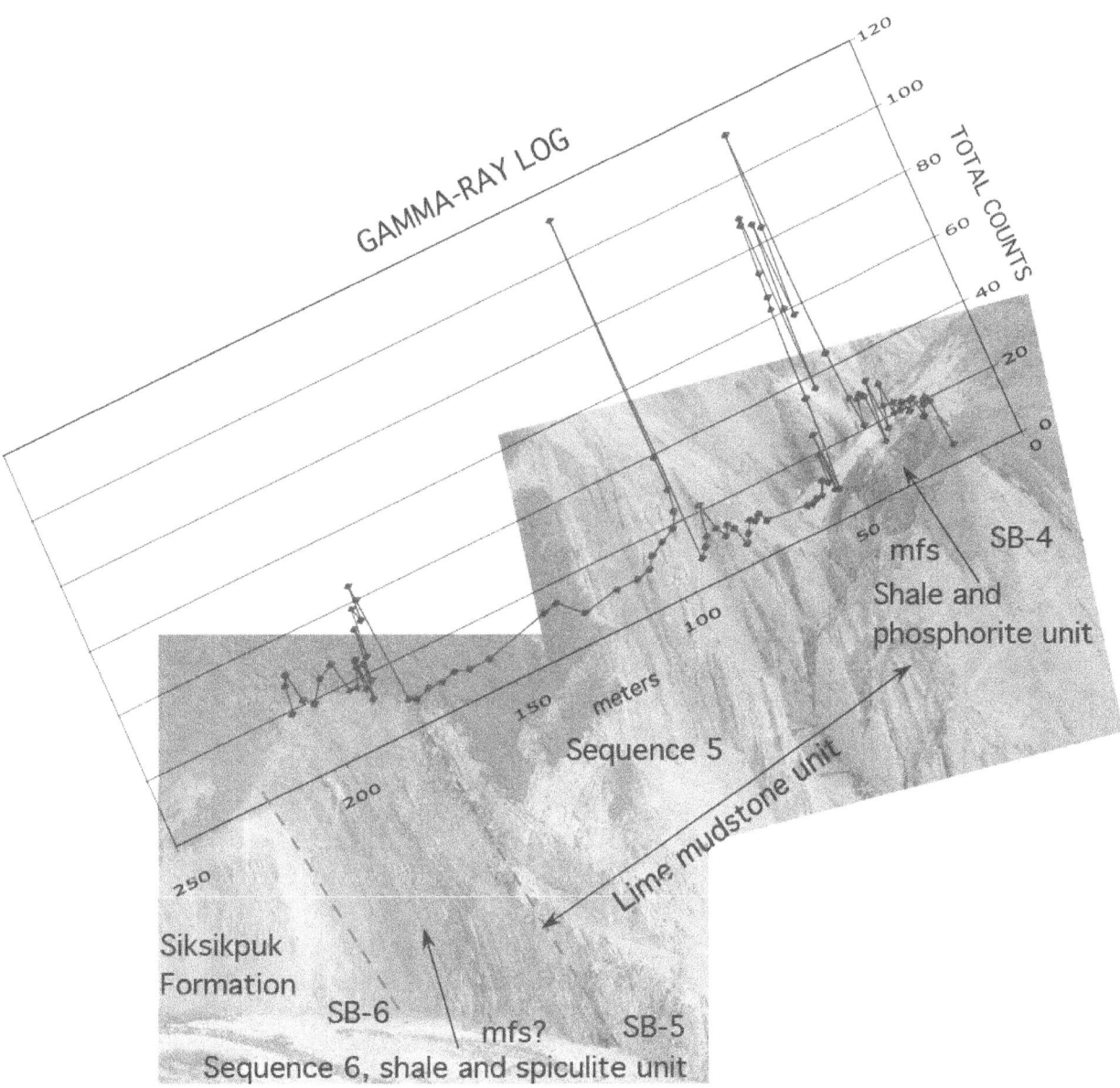

Figure 13. Outcrop photomosaic of upper part of the Skimo Creek section (loc. 1, fig. 2) showing lithologic units, sequence stratigraphy, and gamma-ray response in upper part of the Lisburne Group. Note high gamma-ray response in the shale and phosphorite unit (fig. 3) that records maximum flooding within sequence 5. Another gamma-ray spike in the lime mudstone unit (fig. 3), ~40 m above top of the shale and phosphorite unit (fig. 3), marks a flooding surface associated with a parasequence within sequence 5. Spikes also occur in the shale and spiculite unit (fig. 3) of sequence 6 ("black Lisburne"), indicating ultimate platform drowning.

with equally high TOC contents crop out in parts of the Killik River, Howard Pass, Misheguk Mountain, and De Long Mountains quadrangles farther west (Dumoulin and others, 2004, 2005, 2006b).

Other parts of the Lisburne Group also have some source-rock potential. Shale makes up more than half of the 40-m-thick shale and spiculite unit at Skimo Creek (fig. 2), and although the TOC contents in this unit are lower than in the shale and phosphorite unit, all the samples analyzed contained at least 1.68 weight percent TOC (table 5). These strata form a mappable unit in the study area (fig. 2; Peapples and others, 2007) but appear to have a considerably more limited regional extent than does the shale and phosphorite unit. TOC contents comparable to those in the shale and spiculite unit were measured in several samples of argillaceous limestone and calcareous shale from the nodular limestone and dolostone unit at Tiglukpuk Creek (fig. 2). However, the most organic rich rock types in this unit typically occur as partings and interbeds, only a few centimeters thick, and appear to have a cumulative thickness of a few meters at most.

TOC contents in the shale and phosphorite unit at Skimo Creek (fig. 2) are similar to those in the Kuna Formation and related rocks of the Lisburne Group to the west (Slack and others, 2004a, b). Rock eval data from Lisburne shales, including samples from the study area (fig. 2), show a trend of decreasing yield of pyrolitic hydrocarbons with increasing thermal maturity, indicating that the Lisburne rocks have generated oil and gas (Dumoulin and others, 2005). Extrapolated to low levels of thermal maturity, this trend suggests that these potential Lisburne source rocks are rich in type II and, possibly, type I organic matter (R. Burruss, written commun., 2006).

Organic-rich shale interbeds in the shale and phosphorite unit at Skimo Creek (fig. 2) are also metalliferous and contain as much as 1,690 ppm Cr, 2,831 ppm V, 551 ppm Ni, 4,670 ppm Zn, 108 ppm Mo, 43.5 ppm Ag, and 29 ppb Pd (Dumoulin and others, 2006a; J. Slack, unpub. data, 2007). Lisburne Group phosphatic black shales with high metal contents are geologically and geochemically similar to those that host the Nick Ni-Zn-Mo–platinum-group-element (PGE) deposit (Devonian) in Yukon Territory, Canada, and the Tianeshan Ni-Mo-PGE deposit (Cambrian) in southern China and may be prospective for similar deposits (Dumoulin and others, 2006a, b).

Hydrocarbon Reservoir Facies

Although primary porosity throughout the Lisburne Group is largely occluded by early calcite cement, secondary porosity is well developed in some outcrop and subsurface sections (Bird and Jordan, 1977; Jameson, 1994; Dumoulin and Bird, 2002; Dumoulin and others, 2005). Dolostones that have both secondary porosity and locally notable amounts of dead oil are the best potential hydrocarbon reservoir facies of the Lisburne in the study area (fig. 2). These rocks are distributed discontinuously throughout both the Skimo Creek and Tiglukpuk Creek sections (figs. 3 and 9, respectively), but their lateral continuity is uncertain. Similar strata occur to the east at Shainin Lake

(fig. 2), as well as to the west in the Ivotuk Hills and Red Dog areas (fig. 1; Dumoulin and Harris, 1993; Dumoulin and Bird, 2002; Dumoulin and others, 2004). In the study area, porous dolostones are relatively coarse grained (dolomite crystals, typically 0.1–>1 mm diam), contain relict crinoid ossicles, display large-scale crossbeds, and probably formed as crinoidal grainstones in sand waves and shoals of the midramp to inner ramp. Solid hydrocarbons partly or completely fill some intercrystalline and moldic pores (commonly after crinoid ossicles) in these dolostones, as well as vugs and fractures. Porous dolostones extend through intervals 5 to >20 m thick at several stratigraphic levels in the study area, but the highest porosities are generally concentrated in intervals 1 to 2 m thick. Krynine and others (1950) reported effective porosities as high as 11 percent in the Lisburne Group at Shainin Lake; thin-section observations suggest that maximum porosities in the study area are similar.

Porous dolostones are best developed near the base of the lower dolostone unit and near the top of the middle dolostone and upper dolostone units at Skimo Creek (figs. 2, 3) and near the middle and top of the nodular limestone and dolostone unit at Tiglukpuk Creek (fig. 9). These horizons, which coincide closely with our proposed sequence boundaries, occur just below the tops of sequences 1, 3, and 4 at Skimo Creek and of sequences 2 and 3 at Tiglukpuk Creek, and at stratigraphic levels that likely correspond to the tops of sequences 1 through 3 at Shainin Lake (fig. 2).

Geochemical parameters indicate a good match between oil stains in porous dolostones of the Lisburne Group in the Ivotuk Hills (fig. 1) and organic-rich Lisburne shales interbedded with phosphorites in nearby outcrops (Dumoulin and others, 2005). Thus, solid hydrocarbons in Lisburne dolostones in the study area probably were also sourced by organic-rich Lisburne shales.

Thermal Maturity

Conodonts provide data on the thermal history of the rocks that contain them (Epstein and others, 1977). Color-alteration indices (CAIs) of conodonts from the Lisburne Group in the Skimo Creek section (fig. 3) range from 1–1.5 to 2.5 (table 2). Most assemblages have CAI values of 1.5 to 2.0 or 2.5, indicating that temperatures reached at least 50–100°C (table 6; Epstein and others, 1977; Watts and others, 1994). CAI values in the Tiglukpuk Creek section (fig. 9) are more uniform, slightly lower overall, and range from 1.5 to 2 (table 3). Other Lisburne Group samples collected during this study from thrust sheets south and east of the Skimo thrust sheet have CAI values like those from the Skimo Creek and Tiglukpuk Creek sections, although a few samples have slightly higher CAI values (2 or 2.5–3 at locs. 15, 18, 19, fig. 2; table 4).

Correlation of CAI values with other thermal maturity indices (Bird and others, 1999) indicates that the Lisburne Group in the Skimo and Tiglukpuk thrust sheets reached temperatures mainly within the window for oil generation (CAI values of 1.5–2, table 6). These estimated temperatures agree

Table 5. Total organic-carbon (TOC) contents of samples from the Lisburne Group in the study area.

[See figures 1 and 2 for locations and figures 3 and 9 for stratigraphic columns of the Skimo Creek and Tiglukpuk Creek sections, respectively, in northern Alaska. All samples collected by J.A. Dumoulin except field No. CMD 4617, which was collected by J.M. Kurtak, U.S. Bureau of Land Management. Asterisks, samples analyzed by Activation Laboratories in Ancaster, Ontario, Canada; all other samples analyzed at the U.S. Geological Survey laboratory in Denver, Colo.]

Field No.	Section, unit (subunit)	TOC content (wt pct)	Lithology
TNA 10.6	Tiglukpuk Creek (loc. 2, fig. 2), nodular limestone and dolostone unit (subunit 2).	1.09	Dark-gray argillaceous lime-stone.
TNA18.9	do	1.77	Sooty, black argillaceous lime-stone.
TNA 44.9	Tiglukpuk Creek (loc. 2, fig. 2), nodular limestone and dolostone unit (subunit 3).	1.68	Dark-gray calcareous shale.
TNB 4.5	Tiglukpuk Creek (loc. 2, fig. 2), nodular limestone and dolostone unit (subunit 4).	1.24	Do.
SKB 10	Skimo Creek (loc. 1, fig. 2), shale and phosphorite unit.	8.00	Sooty, calcareous black shale.
SKBo 25	do	5.32*	Do.
SKB 25.4	do	5.54	Do.
SKB 31	do	5.13	Do.
CMD 4617	Tiglukpuk Creek (loc. 7, fig. 2), shale and phosphorite unit	3.16*	Calcareous black phosphorite.
04AD9J	Confusion Creek (loc. 4, fig. 2), shale and phosphorite unit.	2.43*	Do.
CCP 0.4	do	6.38*	Sooty, calcareous, phosphatic black shale.
CCP 1.35	do	8.05*	Do.
CCP 3.4	do	9.43*	Do.
CCP 5.8	do	5.14*	Do.
CCP 5.8A	do	4.19*	Do.
CCP 7.5	do	2.92*	Do.
05AD6E	Monotis Creek (loc. 5, fig. 2), shale and phosphorite unit.	15.0*	Do.
SKA 180.5	Skimo Creek, shale and spiculite unit.	1.79	Calcareous black shale.
SKA 183.5	do	1.68	Do.
SKA 200	do	1.88*	Do.

with those based on vitrinite reflectance and T_{max} data from a
small group of Lisburne samples collected near locality 7 (fig.
2; Johnsson and others, 1999; K. Bird, written commun., 2002).
Vitrinite reflectances of four samples ranged from 0.5 to 1.23,
and T_{max} values for 12 samples ranged from 424 to 452.

Conclusions

Lithofacies and faunal data indicate that the Lisburne
Group in the study area (fig. 2) was deposited in mainly
midramp to outer-ramp environments during late Early Mississippian (Osagean) through Early Pennsylvanian (early Morrowan) time. Sections in two distinct thrust sheets of the Endicott Mountains allochthon that were likely separated by ~12 to
17 km during deposition correlate well but show some facies
differences due to the more landward position of the northern,
Tiglukpuk Creek section (fig. 9) relative to the southern, Skimo
Creek section (fig. 3); the Skimo Creek section is also thicker
(>900 versus ~760 m).

Six chronostratigraphic (probable third order) sequences
can be recognized in the Lisburne Group in the study area (fig.
2), all of which correlate with sequences previously delineated
in the Lisburne farther east. Only the upper part of sequence
1 (Osagean) is exposed in the study area, where it consists
of ~20 m of dolomitized crinoidal supportstone (facies 1B,
table 1) that accumulated in a near-shoal midramp setting.
Sequences 2 through 4 (late Osagean-Meramecian), ~160 to
290 m thick, are characterized by a similar array of lithofacies: muddier strata (facies 2–4) intercalated with grainier
rocks (facies 1A, 1B). Increasing amounts of mud and local,
partially phosphatized firmgrounds and hardgrounds mark the
TSTs in these sequences. Coarsening- and thickening-upward
packages typify the HSTs. Sequence 5 (Chesterian), 100 to
160 m thick, records a significant drowning of the Lisburne
carbonate platform during early Chesterian time. Lime mudstone, organic-rich shale, and various phosphatic strata (facies
5–7) that are notable parts of this sequence accumulated in
a sediment-starved, nutrient-rich setting with at least locally
dysoxic to anoxic bottom conditions. Bioclastic supportstone
(facies 1A, 1B) caps shallowing-upward parasequences in the
HST of this sequence and is considerably more abundant in the
Tiglukpuk Creek section (fig. 9). Sequence 6 (late? Chesterian-
Morrowan), ~40 m thick, documents a second, final drowning
of the Lisburne platform in this area. Shale, lime mudstone,
spiculite, and glauconitic siltstone to grainstone (facies 5, 8,
9) make up this sequence; lithofacies and faunal data indicate
low sedimentation rates. These strata contain significantly less
organic matter and phosphorus than do the rocks of sequence 5,
implying that nutrification and reduced oxygen levels were not
associated with this drowning event. Regional correlations suggest that tectonic factors may have caused the ultimate demise
of the Lisburne carbonate platform in the study area.

The Lisburne Group in the study area (fig. 2) contains
both potential hydrocarbon source and reservoir facies and

Table 6. Temperature ranges for color-alteration indexes (CAIs)
of conodonts in samples from the study area.

[See figure 1 for location of study area in northern Alaska. Temperature data
from Epstein and others (1977) and Watts and others (1994); oil-generation
stages from Bird and others (1999). Temperature ranges for CAI values from
an Arrhenius plot of experimental data; ranges for each value cover heating
durations of 1 to 500 m.y., where upper and lower temperatures in range (for
example, 80°C and 50°C for CAI=1) correspond to 1- and 500-m.y. heating
durations, respectively]

CAI value	Temperature (°C)	Oil generation
1	<50–80	Immature
1.5	50–90	Onset of oil generation
2	60–140	
2.5	100–150	Limit of oil generation
3	120–190	Limit of oil preservation

reached temperatures mainly within the oil window. Calcareous
shale deposited during the TST and early HST of sequence 5
in the Skimo thrust sheet is an excellent potential hydrocarbon
source rock, with a cumulative thickness of >15 m, a lateral
extent of at least 50 km, and consistently high TOC contents
(3–15 weight percent). Dolomitized crinoidal grainstone with
locally abundant secondary porosity is the most prospective
reservoir facies in the Lisburne in the study area; it occurs in
both the Skimo and Tiglukpuk thrust sheets and is best developed in the upper HSTs of sequences 1 through 4. These rocks
have intercrystalline, moldic, vuggy, and fracture porosity
(max ~10 percent) and occur in intervals 5 to >20 m thick that
are of uncertain lateral extent. Dead oil that commonly fills or
lines pores in the dolostones was likely derived from nearby
Lisburne source rocks.

Acknowledgments

We thank the Alaska Division of Geological and Geophysical Surveys and Petro-Canada Oil and Gas for logistical support
of our fieldwork, particularly Ellie Harris and Paige Peapples
(Alaska Division of Geological and Geophysical Surveys), Gil
Mull (Alaska Division of Oil and Gas), and Jeff Bever, Jeff
Lukasic, and Mike McDonough (Petro-Canada Oil and Gas)
for their help and stimulating discussions in the field and office.
Thanks also go to Mark Florence of the Smithsonian Institu-
tion for the loan of thin sections collected by A.K. Armstrong
at Skimo Creek, and to Ken Bird (U.S. Geological Survey) and
Randy Carlson (Kansas Department of Health and Environ-
ment) for their insightful and timely reviews of the manuscript.

References Cited

Adams, K.E., 1991, Permian sedimentation in the north-central Brooks Range, Alaska; implications for tectonic reconstructions: Fairbanks, University of Alaska, M.S. thesis, 122 p.

Adams, K.E., 1994, Columnar sections and lithostratigraphic correlation of the Permian Siksikpuk and Echooka Formations, Northcentral Brooks Range, northern Alaska: Alaska Division of Geological and Geophysical Surveys Public-Data File 94–95.

Armstrong, A.K., and Mamet, B.L., 1977, Carboniferous microfacies, microfossils, and corals, Lisburne Group, Arctic Alaska: U.S. Geological Survey Professional Paper 849, 129 p.

Armstrong, A.K., and Mamet, B.L., 1978, Microfacies of the Carboniferous Lisburne Group, Endicott Mountains, arctic Alaska, *in* Stelck, C.R., and Chatterton, B.D.E., eds., Western and arctic Canadian biostratigraphy: Geological Association of Canada Special Paper 18, p. 333–394.

Armstrong, A.K., Mamet, B.L., and Dutro, J.T., Jr., 1970, Foraminiferal zonation and carbonate facies of Carboniferous (Mississippian and Pennsylvanian) Lisburne Group, central and eastern Brooks Range, Arctic Alaska: American Association of Petroleum Geologists Bulletin, v. 54, no. 5, p. 687–698.

Aurell, M., Badenas, B., Bosence, D.W.J., and Waltham, D.A., 1998, Carbonate production and offshore transport on a Late Jurassic carbonate ramp (Kimmeridgian, Iberian basin, NE Spain); evidence from outcrops and computer modelling, *in* Wright, V.P., and Burchette, T.P., eds., Carbonate ramps; an introduction: Geological Society of London Special Publication 149, p. 137–162.

Azeredo, A.C., 1998, Geometry and facies dynamics of Middle Jurassic carbonate ramp sandbodies, West-Central Portugal, *in* Wright, V.P., and Burchette, T.P., eds., Carbonate ramps; an introduction: Geological Society of London Special Publication 149, p. 281–314.

Bird, K.J., 1988, Structure-contour and isopach maps of the National Petroleum Reserve in Alaska, *in* Gryc, G., ed., Geology and exploration of the National Petroleum Reserve in Alaska, 1974–1982: U.S. Geological Survey Professional Paper 1399, p. 355–377.

Bird, K.J., Burruss, R.C., and Pawlewicz, M.J., 1999, Thermal maturity, *in* ANWR assessment team, ed., The oil and gas resource potential of the 1002 Area, Arctic National Wildlife Refuge, Alaska: U.S. Geological Survey Open-File Report 98–34, p. V1–V64.

Bird, K.J., and Jordan, C.F., 1977, Lisburne Group (Mississippian and Pennsylvanian), potential major hydrocarbon objective of Arctic Slope, Alaska: American Association of Petroleum Geologists Bulletin, v. 61, no. 9, p. 1493–1512.

Bowsher, A.L., and Dutro, J.T., Jr., 1957, The Paleozoic section in the Shainin Lake area, central Brooks Range, Alaska: U.S. Geological Survey Professional Paper 303–A, 39 p.

Brosgé, W.P., and Armstrong, A.K., 1977, Lithologic logs of Lisburne Group in Lawrence Livermore Laboratory Drill Holes 1 and 2, Confusion Creek, Chandler Lake quadrangle, northern Alaska: U.S. Geological Survey Open-File Report 77–26, 11 p.

Brosgé, W.P., Reiser, H.N., Dutro, J.T., Jr., and Detterman, R.L., 1981, Organic geochemical data for Mesozoic and Paleozoic shales, central and eastern Brooks Range, Alaska: U.S. Geological Survey Open-File Report 81–551, 17 p.

Brosgé, W.P., Reiser, H.N., Patton, W.W., Jr., and Mangus, M.D., 1960, Geologic map of the Killik-Anaktuvuk Rivers region, Brooks Range, Alaska: U.S. Geological Survey Open-File Report, 2 sheets, scale 1:96,000.

Burchette, T.P., and Wright, V.P., 1992, Carbonate ramp depositional systems: Sedimentary Geology, v. 79, no. 1–4, p. 3–57.

Dumoulin, J.A., and Bird, K.J., 2001, Stratigraphy and lithofacies of Lisburne Group carbonate rocks (Carboniferous-Permian) in the National Petroleum Reserve-Alaska, *in* Houseknecht, D.W., ed., NPRA Core Workshop; petroleum plays and systems in the National Petroleum Reserve-Alaska: Society for Sedimentary Geology (SEPM) Core Workshop 21, Denver, Colo., 2001, p. 141–166.

Dumoulin, J.A., and Bird, K.J., 2002, Lithofacies and stratigraphy of the Lisburne and Etivluk Groups in the Lisburne 1 well and adjacent outcrops, central Brooks Range, Alaska [abs.]: American Association of Petroleum Geologists Bulletin, v. 86, no. 6, p. 1142.

Dumoulin, J.A., Burruss, R.C., Lillis, P.G., and Parris, T.M., 2005, New field and geochemical evidence on the nature and extent of the Lisburne petroleum system (Northern Alaska) [abs.]: Geological Society of America Abstracts with Programs, v. 37, no. 4, p. 93.

Dumoulin, J.A., and Harris, A.G., 1993, Lithofacies and conodonts of Carboniferous strata in the Ivotuk Hills, western Brooks Range, Alaska, *in* Dusel-Bacon, C., and Till, A.B., eds., Geologic studies in Alaska by the U.S. Geological Survey during 1992: U.S. Geological Survey Bulletin 2068, p. 31–47.

Dumoulin, J.A., Harris, A.G., Blome, C.D., and Young, L.E., 2004, Depositional settings, correlation, and age of Carboniferous rocks in the western Brooks Range, Alaska: Economic Geology, v. 99, no. 7, p. 1355–1384.

Dumoulin, J.A., Harris, A.G., and Schmidt, J.M., 1993, Deep-water lithofacies and conodont faunas of the Lisburne Group, western Brooks Range, Alaska, *in* Dusel-Bacon, C., and Till, A.B., eds., Geologic studies in Alaska by the U.S. Geological Survey during 1992: U.S. Geological Survey Bulletin 2068, p. 12–30.

Dumoulin, J.A., Harris, A.G., Slack, J.F., and Whalen, M.T., 2006a, Phosphatic rocks of the Lisburne Group in the southern NPRA and adjacent areas [abs.]: Alaska Miners Association Annual Convention Abstracts, p. 12–14.

Dumoulin, J.A., Watts, K.F., and Harris, A.G., 1997, Stratigraphic contrasts and tectonic relationships between Carboniferous successions in the Trans-Alaska Crustal Transect corridor and adjacent areas, northern Alaska: Journal of Geophysical Research, v. 102, no. B9, p. 20709–20726.

Dumoulin, J.A., Whalen, M.T., Harris, A.G., and Slack, J.F., 2006b, Paleogeographic and metallogenic implications of phosphatic rocks in the Lisburne Group (Permian-Carboniferous), northern Alaska [abs.]: Geological Society of America Abstracts with Programs, v. 38, no. 5, p. 85.

Dunham, R.J., 1962, Classification of carbonate rocks according to depositional texture, *in* Ham, W.E., ed., Classification of carbonate rocks—a symposium: American Association of Petroleum Geologists Memoir 1, p. 108–121.

Dutro, J.T., Jr., 1987, Revised megafossil biostratigraphic zonation for the Carboniferous of northern Alaska, *in* Tailleur, I.L. and Weimer, P., eds., Alaskan North Slope Geology: Society of Economic Geologists and Mineralogists, Pacific Section Book 50, v. 1, p. 359–364.

Embry, A.F., III, and Klovan, J.E., 1972, Absolute water depth limits of Late Devonian paleoecological zones: Geologische Rundschau, v. 61, no. 2, p. 672–686.

Epstein, A.G., Epstein, J.B., and Harris, L.D., 1977, Conodont color alteration—an index to organic metamorphism: U.S. Geological Survey Professional Paper 995, 27 p.

Franseen, E.K., Pray, L.C., and Fekete, T.E., 1987, Mid-Permian shelf margin erosion surfaces, western escarpment, Guadalupe Mountains, Texas [abs.]: American Association of Petroleum Geologists Bulletin, v. 71, no. 5, p. 557.

Gomez-Perez, I., Fernandez-Mendiola, P.A., and Garcia-Mondejar, J., 1998, Constructional dynamics for a Lower Cretaceous carbonate ramp (Gorbea Massif, North Iberia), *in* Wright, V.P., and Burchette, T.P., eds., Carbonate ramps; an introduction: Geological Society of London Special Publication 149, p. 229–252.

Gordon, M., Jr., 1957, Mississippian cephalopods of northern and eastern Alaska: U.S. Geological Survey Professional Paper 283, 61 p.

Gradstein, F.M., Ogg, J.G., and Smith, A.G., 2004, A geologic time scale 2004: Cambridge, U.K., Cambridge University Press, 589 p.

Jameson, J., 1994, Models of porosity formation and their impact on reservoir description, Lisburne Field, Prudhoe Bay, Alaska: American Association of Petroleum Geologists Bulletin, v. 78, no. 11, p. 1651–1678.

Johnsson, M.J., Evans, K.R., and Marshall, H.A., 1999, Thermal maturity of sedimentary rocks in Alaska; digital resources: U.S. Geological Survey Digital Data Series DDS–54, CD–ROM [URL http://pubs.usgs.gov/dds/dds-54/ (accessed Oct. 26, 2007)].

Kelley, J.S., 1988, Preliminary geologic map of the Chandler Lake quadrangle, Alaska: U.S. Geological Survey Open-File Report 88–42, 2 sheets, scale 1:125,000.

Kelley, J.S., 1990, Generalized geologic map of the Chandler Lake quadrangle, north-central Alaska: U.S. Geological Survey Miscellaneous Field Studies Map MF–2144–A, scale 1:250,000.

Kelley, J.S., and Brosgé, W.P., 1995, Geologic framework of a transect of the central Brooks Range; regional relations and an alternative to the Endicott Mountains Allochthon: American Association of Petroleum Geologists Bulletin, v. 79, no. 8, p. 1087–1116.

Kelley, K.D., and Jennings, S., 2004, Barite and Zn-Pb-Ag deposits in the Red Dog District, western Brooks Range, Northern Alaska; preface: Economic Geology, v. 99, no. 7, p. 1267–1280.

Krumhardt, A.P., Harris, A.G., and Watts, K.F., 1996, Litostratigraphy, microlithofacies, and conodont biostratigraphy and biofacies of the Wahoo Limestone (Carboniferous), eastern Sadlerochit Mountains, northeast Brooks Range, Alaska: U.S. Geological Survey Professional Paper 1568, 71 p.

Krynine, P.D., Folk, R.L., and Rosenfeld, M.A., 1950, Porosity and petrography of Lisburne Limestone samples from the Kanayut, Nanushuk and Itkillik Lakes area, *with a discussion of* The distribution of porous zones in the Lisburne Limestone, by A.L. Bowsher: U.S. Geological Survey open-file report (Geological Investigations of Naval Petroleum Reserve No. 4 Special Report 17), 18 p.

Kurtak, J.M., Hicks, R.W., Werdon, M.B., Meyer, M.P., and Mull, C.G., 1995, Mineral investigations in the Colville Mining District and southern National Petroleum Reserve in Alaska: U.S. Bureau of Mines Open-File Report 8–95, 217 p.

Lasemi, Z., Norby, R.D., and Treworgy, J.D., 1998, Depositional facies and sequence stratigraphy of a Lower Carboniferous bryozoan-crinoidal carbonate ramp in the Illinois Basin, mid-continent USA, *in* Wright, V.P., and Burchette, T.P., eds., Carbonate ramps; an introduction: Geological Society of London Special Publication 149, p. 369–395.

McGee, M.M., 2004, Carboniferous Lisburne Group carbonates of the Porcupine Lake Valley; implications for surface to subsurface sequence stratigraphy, paleogeography, and paleoclimatology: Fairbanks, University of Alaska, Ph.D. thesis, 454 p.

Moore, D.W., Young, L.E., Modene, J.S., and Plahuta, J.T., 1986, Geologic setting and genesis of the Red Dog zinc-lead-silver deposit, western Brooks Range, Alaska: Economic Geology, v. 81, no. 7, p. 1696–1727.

Oldow, J.S., Seidensticker, C.M., Phelps, J.C., Julian, F.E., Gottschalk, R.R., Boler, K.W., Handschy, J.W., and Avé Lallemant, H.G., 1987, Balanced cross sections through the central Brooks Range and North Slope, Arctic Alaska: Tulsa, Okla., American Association of Petroleum Geologists, 19 p., 8 plates, scale 1:200,000.

Patton, W.W., Jr., and Matzko, J.J., 1959, Phosphate deposits in northern Alaska: U.S. Geological Survey Professional Paper 302–A, 17 p.

Peapples, P.R., Wallace, W.K., Wartes, M.A., Swenson, R.F., Mull, C.G., Dumoulin, J.A., Harris, E.E., Finzel, E.S., Reifenstuhl, R.R., and Loveland, A.M., 2007, Geologic map of the Siksikpuk River area, Chandler Lake quadrangle, Alaska: Alaska Division of Geological and Geophysical Surveys Preliminary Interpretive Report 2007–1, scale 1:63,360.

Poole, F.G., and Sandberg, C.A., 1991, Mississippian paleogeography and conodont biostratigraphy of the Western United States, *in* Cooper, J.D., and Stevens, C.H., eds., Paleozoic paleogeography of the Western United States—II: Society of Economic Paleontologists and Mineralogists, Pacific Section Field Trip Guidebook, v. 67, p. 107–136.

Pray, L.C., Crawford, G.A., and Harris, M.T., 1980, Early Guadalupian (Permian) bank margin erosion surfaces, Guadalupe Mountains, Texas [abs.]: American Association of Petroleum Geologists Bulletin, v. 64, no. 5, p. 768.

Purnell, M.A., 1992, Conodonts of the lower Border Group and equivalent strata (Lower Carboniferous) in northern Cumbria and the Scottish Borders, U.K.: Royal Ontario Museum Life Sciences Contributions 156, 78 p.

Scholle, P.A., Bebout, D.G., and Moore, C.H., 1983, Carbonate depositional environments: American Association of Petroleum Geologists Memoir 33, 708 p.

Siok, J.P., 1985, Geologic history of the Siksikpuk Formation on the Endicott Mountains and Picnic Creek allochthons, north-central Brooks Range, Alaska: Fairbanks, University of Alaska, M.S. thesis, 253 p.

Slack, J.F., Dumoulin, J.A., Schmidt, J.M., Young, L.E., and Rombach, C.S., 2004a, Paleozoic sedimentary rocks in the Red Dog Zn-Pb-Ag district and vicinity, western Brooks Range, Alaska; provenance, deposition, and metallogenic significance: Economic Geology, v. 99, no. 7, p. 1385–1414.

Slack, J.F., Schmidt, J.M., and Dumoulin, J.A., 2004b, Whole rock geochemical data for Paleozoic sedimentary rocks of the western Brooks Range, Alaska: U.S. Geological Survey Open-File Report 2004–1371 [URL http://pubs.usgs.gov/of/2004/1371/].

Tissot, B.P., and Welte, D.H., 1984, Petroleum formation and occurrence (2d ed.): Berlin, Springer-Verlag, 699 p.

van Wagoner, J.C., Posamentier, H.W., Mitchum, R.M., Vail, P.R., Sarg, J.F., Loutit, T.S., and Hardenbol, J., 1988, An overview of the fundamentals of sequence stratigraphy, *in* Wilgus, C.K., Hastings, B.S., Kendall, C.G.S.C., Posamentier, H.W., Ross, C.A., and van Wagoner, J.C., eds., Sea-level change; an integrated approach: Society for Sedimentary Geology (SEPM) Special Publication 42, p. 39–45.

Watts, K.F., Harris, A.G., Carlson, R.C., Eckstein, M.K., Gruzlovic, P.D., Imm, T.A., Krumhardt, A.P., Lasota, D.K., Morgan, S.K., Enos, Paul, Goldstein, R., Dumoulin, J.A., and Mamet, B., 1994, Analysis of reservoir heterogeneities due to shallowing-upward cycles in carbonate rocks of the Upper Mississippian and Pennsylvanian Wahoo limestone of northeastern Alaska: U.S. Department of Energy report under contract DE–AC22–89BC14471, 433 p.

Whalen, M.T., Dumoulin, J.A., Lukasic, J.J., McGee, M.M., White, J.G., and Toendel, T.D., 2005, Carboniferous phosphorite deposition and carbonate platform drowning, Lisburne Group, central Brooks Range, Alaska [abs.]: Geological Society of America Abstracts with Programs, v. 37, no. 4, p. 93.

Whalen, M.T., Dumoulin, J.A., Lukasic, J.J., and White, J.G., 2006, Simultaneous carbonate platform progradation and drowning, Lisburne Group, eastern and central Brooks Range, Alaska [abs.]: Geological Society of America Abstracts with Programs, v. 38, no. 5, p. 86.

White, J.G, and Whalen, M.T., 2006, Accumulation history, facies analysis, and reservoir potential of the Carboniferous Lisburne Group, upper Nanushuk River drainage, central Brooks Range, Alaska [abs.]: Geological Society of America Abstracts with Programs, v. 38, no. 5, p. 85.

Wilson, J.L., and Jordan, C., 1983, Middle shelf, *in* Scholle, P.A., Bebout, D.G., and Moore, C.H., eds., Carbonate depositional environments: American Association of Petroleum Geologists Memoir 33, p. 297–344.

Wright, V.P., and Burchette, T.P., 1998, Carbonate ramps; an introduction: Geological Society of London Special Publication 149, 465 p.

Young, L.E., 2004, A geologic framework for mineralization in the western Brooks Range, Alaska: Economic Geology, v. 99, no. 7, p. 1281–1306.

Tables 2–4

Table 2.   Conodont samples from the Skimo Creek section, northern Alaska.

[See figure 2 for locations. All samples collected by J.A. Dumoulin unless otherwise indicated; all faunas identified by A.G. Harris. CAI, conodont color-alteration index; indet., indeterminate; no., number]

Field No., (USGS colln. no.), stratigraphic unit, and position	Quadrangle, latitude N., longitude W.	Facies (table 1), lithology, and sequence position	Conodont fauna	Age	CAI	Conodont biofacies and depositional environment	Remarks
SKIMO 1 (33739-PC) Lisburne Group, lower dolostone unit; sample from 14 m above base of section, which is lowest exposure of the Lisburne on the north limb of Skimo anticline.	Chandler Lake B-4 68°17.00', 151°55.53'	Facies 1B Sample from near top of an 18-m-thick interval of dolostone with local vuggy porosity and possible large-scale crossbeds. Some pores contain dead oil; porosity is greatest near base of interval. Thin section is completely dolomitized skeletal grainstone with relict crinoid and lesser bryozoan fragments. Sequence 1, HST	6 Pa element fragments *Bispathodus stabilis* Branson and Mehl or *Bi. utahensis* Sandberg and Gutschick 1 Pa element *Hindeodus crassidentatus* (Branson and Mehl) or aff. *Hi. crassidentatus* *Kladognathus* sp. indet. 9 M, 1 Sa, and 4 Sb-Sc mostly incomplete element fragments (2 robust M elements nearly complete) Unassigned elements: 3 Pb 166 indet. bar, blade, and platform fragments	Early, but not earliest, Mississippian (middle Kinderhookian-Osagean).	2.5	Biofacies indeterminate (too few generically identifiable conodonts); lithology, species association, and condition of conodonts (mostly broken) indicate deposition within or postmortem transport from a relatively high energy, shallow-water, normal-marine setting.	Sample from section SKC in west-central part of sec. 28, T. 13 S., R. 1 E., elevation ~2,600 ft; measured mostly along east side of Skimo Creek. Heavy-mineral concentrate contains phosphatized and phosphatic bioclasts (mainly brachiopods and ichthyoliths, lesser fenestrate bryozoans and gastropod and peleeypod steinkerns, and dolomitized and phosphatized pelmatozoan fragments). 5.8 kg of rock was processed. Sample collected by Jeff Lukasic, Petro-Canada Oil & Gas.
SKIMO 2 (33740-PC) Lisburne Group, nodular limestone unit; sample from ~55 m above base of section.	Chandler Lake B-4 Close to (slightly north of) 68°17.00', 151°55.53'	Facies 1B Sample from ~2 m above base of a 7.4-m-thick interval of skeletal supportstone that occurs within a thick sequence of cherty, fine-grained, nodular limestone. Sample is medium-light- to medium-gray (slightly brown) limestone that weathers light olive gray. Fetid, packed crinoid grainstone, with crinoid ossicles (max 5 mm diam) and spiriferid brachiopods (max 3 cm diam). Sequence 2, TST	*Hindeodus crassidentatus* (Branson and Mehl) or aff. *Hi. crassidentatus* 18 mostly incomplete Pa and 1 Sc elements *Kladognathus* sp. indet. 1 M and 1 incomplete Sb-Sc elements 1 unassigned Pb element 38 indet. bar, blade, and platform fragments	Early, but not earliest, Mississippian (middle Kinderhookian-Osagean).	2.0-2.5	Postmortem transport within or from a hindeodid biofacies; a shallow-water depositional setting.	Heavy-mineral concentrate is chiefly phosphatic and phosphatized bioclasts (mainly ichthyoliths, lesser phosphatized and phosphatic brachiopods, and rare bryozoan fragments). 4.05 kg of rock was processed. Sample collected by Jeff Lukasic, Petro-Canada Oil & Gas.
SKC 101.1 (33771-PC) Lisburne Group, nodular limestone unit; sample from 101.1 m above base of section.	Chandler Lake B-4 68°17.375', 151°55.118'	Facies 1A Sample from top of a 1.4-m-thick interval of crinoid supportstone (light gray weathering, light gray to white limestone) in 10- to 30-cm-thick beds. Thin section is partly dolomitized crinoid grainstone with bryozoan and brachiopod fragments, algae, foraminifers, and ostracodes (some articulated). Sequence 2, TST	3 complete to incomplete Pa elements cf. *Bispathodus stabilis* (Branson and Mehl) 1 M element fragment of *Idioprioniodus*? sp. Unassigned elements: 1 M and 1 Sc 1 indet. fragment	Early Mississippian (Kinderhookian-Osagean).	1.5-2.0	Indeterminate (too few conodonts).	Heavy-mineral concentrate contains phosphatic and phosphatized bioclasts (common and diverse ichthyoliths, phosphatized bryozoan fragments, rare ostracode and gastropod steinkerns, scarce phosphatic brachiopod fragments, and rare bryozoan pearls). 6.75 kg of rock was processed.

Table 2. Conodont samples from the Skimo Creek section, northern Alaska.—Continued

[See figure 2 for locations. All samples collected by J.A. Dumoulin unless otherwise indicated; all faunas identified by A.G. Harris. CAI, conodont color-alteration index; indet., indeterminate; no., number]

Field No., (USGS colln. no.), stratigraphic unit, and position	Quadrangle, latitude N., longitude W.	Facies (table 1), lithology, and sequence position	Conodont fauna	Age	CAI	Conodont biofacies and depositional environment	Remarks
SKIMO 3 (33741-PC) Lisburne Group, nodular limestone unit; sample from ~180 m above base of section.	Chandler Lake B-4 Close to (slightly north of) 68°17.375', 151°55.118'	Facies 1A Sample from interval, several meters thick, of dark-gray limestone (crinoidal packstone) with colonial coral fragments as large as 6 cm in diameter. Thin section is skeletal-peloidal packstone-grainstone with a large coral fragment, as well as gastropods, crinoids, ostracodes, foraminifers, and algae. Sequence 2. HST	*Cavusgnathus hudsoni* (Metcalfe) 10 Pa. 1 M, and 1 Sc elements (the presence of a notch produced by the offset of the free blade toward the platform and the small number of free blade denticles distinguish these elements from *Cav. unicornis* aff. *Hindeodus crassidentatus* 3 Pa and 1 Sb elements *Kladognathus* sp. indet. 1 Sa, 1 Sb-Sc element fragments 1 S element *Synclydognathus geminus* (Hinde) 11 indet. bar, blade, and platform fragments	latest Early–earliest Late Mississippian (very late Osagean–very early Meramecian)	2.5	Postmortem transport within or from a cavusgnathid biofacies; a shallow-water depositional setting. *C. hudsoni* is typical of warm, shallow-water sequences that may contain evaporites.	Heavy-mineral concentrate contains abundant composite phosphatized carbonate rock fragments and common bioclasts (including phosphatic brachiopod fragments, ichthyoliths, phosphatized bryozoan fragments, and 1 pelmatozoan ossicle). 4.61 kg of rock was processed. Sample collected by Jeff Lukasic, Petro-Canada Oil & Gas.
SKD 30 (33742-PC) Lisburne Group, middle dolostone unit; sample from ~330 m above base of composite section.	Chandler Lake B-4 68°17.490', 151°55.198'	Facies 4? Medium-brownish-gray limestone that weathers brown (fine- to medium-grained skeletal packstone with crinoids, ostracodes, and solitary rugose corals) in centimeter- to decimeter-thick beds. Part of a 5-m-thick cycle that grades upward from thin-bedded, slightly cherty lime mudstone-wackestone to thicker bedded supзорstone with no chert. Sample from ~1 m below top of cycle. Thin section s skeletal packstone with crinoids, coral fragments, ostracodes, notable foraminifers, and minor dolomite rhombs. Sequence 3. TST	1 complete Pa element *Cavusgnathus regularis* Youngquist and Miller	middle Late Mississippian (late Meramecian–very early Chesterian). Upper age limit of collection constrained by age of conodonts in overlying samples.	~2.5	Indeterminate: too few conodonts.	Base of section SKD is separated from top of section SKC by ~100 m of cover: NW1/4 sec. 28. T. 13 S., R. 1 E. Most samples from west side of creek. Heavy-mineral concentrate contains abundant undissolved composite dolomitic and slightly phosphatic bioclastic grains, minor dolomitized gastropod and ostracode steinkerns and dolomitized pelmatozoan ossicles, and rare thin phosphatic shell fragments and ichthyoliths. 6.4 kg of rock was processed.
SKD 53 (33772-PC) Lisburne Group, middle dolostone unit; sample from ~353 m above base of composite section.	Chandler Lake B-4 Close to but slightly north of 68°17.490', 151°55.198'	Facies 4? Brownish-gray, very fine grained limestone that weathers light gray to medium gray; skeletal packstone with crinoids and rugose corals. Thin section s partly dolomitized crinoidal packstone(?) with a few brachiopod and ostracode fragments. Sequence 3. HST	1 juvenile Pa element *Cavusgnathus* sp. Unassigned elements: 3 juvenile Pa, 2 M, and 2 Sc 28 indet. bar, blade, and platform fragments	middle Late Mississippian (late Meramecian–very early Chesterian). Upper age limit of collection constrained by age of conodonts in overlying samples.	1.5	Indeterminate (too few generically determinate conodonts).	Heavy-mineral concentrate is chiefly phosphatic and phosphatized bioclasts including, in order of decreasing abundance, bryozoans, ichthyoliths, and pelmatozoans. 6.5 kg of rock was processed.

Table 2. Conodont samples from the Skimo Creek section, northern Alaska.—Continued

[See figure 2 for locations. All samples collected by J.A. Dumoulin unless otherwise indicated; all faunas identified by A.G. Harris. CAI, conodont color-alteration index; indet., indeterminate; no., number]

Field No., (USGS colln. no.), stratigraphic unit, and position	Quadrangle, latitude N., longitude W.	Facies (table 1), lithology, and sequence position	Conodont fauna	Age	CAI	Conodont biofacies and depositional environment	Remarks
SKD 130 (33743-PC) Lisburne Group, middle dolostone unit; sample from ~430 m above base of composite section.	Chandler Lake B-4 Close to but slightly south of 68°17.566', 151°55.179'	Facies 1 Medium-light-gray dolomitic limestone that weathers pinkish gray to light brownish gray; skeletal supportstone with notable crinoid ossicles. Thin section is crinoidal packstone with brachiopod fragments and scarce phosphatic bioclasts in a dolomitic cherty matrix. Sequence 3, HST	*Gnathodus* sp. indet. 2 juvenile Pa and 1 M elements *Hindeodus* sp. indet. 2 incomplete Pa elements *Kladognathus* sp. 3 M and 6 Sb-Sc element fragments 447 small indet. bar, blade, and platform fragments Most conodonts are coated with or invaded by organic matter.	Faunule indicates a late Kinderhookian through Chesterian age, but underlying and overlying samples in the section restrict age to middle Late Mississippian (late Meramecian–very early Chesterian).	2.0-2.5	Biofacies indeterminate (too few generically identifiable conodonts): abundance of small conodont fragments indicates a winnow.	Heavy-mineral concentrate is chiefly composite phosphatic, partly dolomitic carbonate grains, with minor medium- to fine-sand-size phosphatic brachiopod fragments and 5 ichthyoliths. 4.93 kg of rock was processed.
SKD 157 Lisburne Group, middle dolostone unit; sample from ~457 m above base of composite section.	Chandler Lake B-4 68°17.566', 151°55.179'	Facies 1 Crinoidal grainstone; some crinoid ossicles as large as 1.5 cm in diameter. Thin section is dolostone with crinoid and bryozoan fragments. Sequence 3, HST	1 indet. bar or blade fragment	Underlying and overlying samples in the section restrict age to middle Late Mississippian (late Meramecian–very early Chesterian).	2.0-2.5	Indeterminate (too few conodonts).	Heavy-mineral concentrate contains phosphatized grains, common phosphatic brachiopod fragments (mostly medium sand size), and 1 ichthyolith. 6.05 kg of rock was processed.
SKD 500 Lisburne Group, middle dolostone unit; sample from ~480 m above base of composite section.	Chandler Lake B-4 Close to but slightly north of 68°17.566', 151°55.179'	Facies 4? Medium-light-gray limestone that weathers light brownish gray (crinoidal supportstone). Thin section is skeletal packstone containing 20-40 percent dolomite; bioclasts are crinoid, brachiopod, and ostracode fragments. Sequence 3, HST	No conodonts or other phosphatic or phosphatized fossils were found.				6.4 kg of rock was processed.
SKD 263 (33773-PC) Lisburne Group, upper dolostone unit; sample from ~563 m above base of composite section.	Chandler Lake B-4 68°17.65', 151°54.97'	Facies 4 Brownish-gray, very fine grained limestone that weathers medium to light gray; skeletal packstone with crinoids and rugose corals. Thin section is partly dolomitized crinoidal wackestone-packstone with brachiopod and bryozoan fragments. Sequence 4, TST	1 juvenile and 1 adult Pa element posterior fragments *Cavusgnathus* sp. indet. 1 Sa element *Synclydognathus geminus* (Hinde) 1 unassigned Sa element 4 indet. bar, blade, and platform fragments	middle Late Mississippian (late Meramecian–very early Chesterian); age restricted by age of conodonts in overlying beds.	1.5-2.0	Indeterminate (too few generically determinate conodonts); species present indicate a relatively shallow-water depositional setting.	Sample from near top of major buttress, ~43 m above base of gorge and just north of point where gorge widens out. Heavy-mineral concentrate contains abundant organic-rich silt and mud, long thin pyritized spicules, minor pale-purple fluorite, and phosphatized bryozoan fragments. 6.0 kg of rock was processed.

Table 2. Conodont samples from the Skimo Creek section, northern Alaska.—Continued

[See figure 2 for locations. All samples collected by J.A. Dumoulin unless otherwise indicated; all faunas identified by A.G. Harris. CAI, conodont color-alteration index; indet., indeterminate; no., number]

Field No., (USGS colln. no.), stratigraphic unit, and position	Quadrangle, latitude N., longitude W.	Facies (table 1), lithology, and sequence position	Conodont fauna	Age	CAI	Conodont biofacies and depositional environment	Remarks
SKD 363 (33774-PC) Lisburne Group, upper dolostone unit; sample from ~663 m above base of composite section.	Chandler Lake B–4 68°17.70', 151°54.97'	Facies 1B Pinkish-gray-weathering, light-brownish-gray limestone; skeletal supportstone with crinoids and bryozoans, in 30-cm-thick beds. Thin section is partially dolomitized crinoidal supportstone with bryozoan fragments, algae, and a few micritic intraclasts. Sequence 4, HST	1 Pa element fragment *Cavusgnathus* sp. 3 Sa element fragments *Kladognathus* sp. *Synchlognathus geminus* (Hinde) 1 Pa and 1 Sc elements Unassigned elements: 2 M, 1 Sa, and 1 Sc 52 indet. bar, blade, and platform fragments	middle Late Mississippian (late Meramecian–very early Chesterian); age restricted by age of conodonts in overlying beds.	1.5–2.0	Indeterminate (too few generically determinate conodonts); species present indicate a relatively shallow water depositional setting.	Sample from north edge of sec. 28, T. 13 S., R. 1 E., elevation ~2,600 ft., west side of creek, within gorge. Heavy-mineral concentrate contains phosphatized bioclasts (mainly bryozoans) and minor white fluorite. 6.0 kg of rock was processed.
SKA 19 (33744-PC) Lisburne Group, upper dolostone unit; sample from ~706 m above base of composite section.	Chandler Lake B–4 68°17.722', 151°55.130'	Facies 1 Sample from a 4-m-thick interval of chert (skeletal wackestone-packstone) and dolostone (skeletal supportstone?). Chert beds thin upward from 30 to 10 cm; dolostone beds thicken upward from 10 to 3 cm. Sample is light-gray, fine-grained dolostone that weathers gray-brown, with 5–10 percent porosity (small vugs) and local dead oil. Thin section is dolomite mosaic with a few relict crinoids. Sequence 4, HST	1 large Pa element *Cavusgnathus convexus* Rexroad 1 anterior Pa element fragment *Cavusgnathus* sp. indet. 2 indet. bar, blade, or platform fragments	middle Late Mississippian (late Meramecian–very early Chesterian). Overlying collections restrict upper part of age range to very early Chesterian.	2.0 or 2.5 (very large conodonts)	Indeterminate (too few conodonts); likely a relatively shallow water depositional setting.	Base of section SKA is separated from top of section SKD by a few meters of cover; SW1/4 sec. 21, T.13 S., R. 1 E. Most samples from east side of Skimo Creek. 6.4 kg of rock was processed.
SKBo 20A (33775-PC) Lisburne Group, shale and phosphorite unit; sample from ~730 m above base of composite section.	Chandler Lake B–4 68°17.773', 151°54.609'	Facies 5 Sample is ovoid concretion (36 cm diam) of medium-dark-gray-weathering, dark-gray to black, very sooty, fetid, fine-grained limestone in black shale; from ~5 m below conspicuous phosphorite bed. Thin section is calcareous spiculite (some spicules are pyritized) with ~5–20 percent phosphatic clasts and bioclasts and a few pelecypod(?) fragments; matrix is fine grained mixture of carbonate (partly dolomite?) and organic material. Sequence 5, HST	10 Pa elements *Gnathodus texanus* Roundy 2 juvenile Pa elements likely *Gn. texanus* 3 incomplete Pa elements *Gnathodus* sp. indet. 2 Pa elements *Rhachistognathus prolixus* Baesemann and Lane Unassigned elements: 3 M (3 morphotypes), 1 Pb, and 3 Sc (3 morphotypes) 60 indet. bar, blade, and platform fragments Conodonts are invaded and (or) partly or largely covered with adventitious organic matter, making precise CAI determination somewhat difficult.	middle Late Mississippian (early Chesterian). Overlapping range of *Gnathodus texanus* and *Rhachistognathus prolixus* restricts age of this collection to the *Gnathodus bilineatus*–Upper *Cavusgnathus* Zone; upper age limit is further constrained by an overlying collection.	~1.0 or 1.5	Postmortem transport as a winnow into relatively deep water; nearly all conodonts are small adults and (or) juveniles. Very organic-rich sample.	Sample from box canyon 0.5 mi east of canyon in which main Skimo Creek section was measured; south-central edge of sec. 21, T. 13 S., R. 1 E., elevation ~2,700 ft. Sample collected from a level equivalent to ~23 m above base of section SKB. Heavy-mineral concentrate contains phosphatized bryozoan fragments and lesser thin, pyritized spicules. 6.0 kg of rock was processed.

Table 2. Conodont samples from the Skimo Creek section, northern Alaska.—Continued

[See figure 2 for locations. All samples collected by J.A. Dumoulin unless otherwise indicated; all faunas identified by A.G. Harris. CAI, conodont color-alteration index; indet, indeterminate; no., number]

Field No., (USGS colln. no.), stratigraphic unit, and position	Quadrangle, latitude N., longitude W.	Facies (table 1), lithology, and sequence position	Conodont fauna	Age	CAI	Conodont biofacies and depositional environment	Remarks
SKB 28.5 (33745-PC) Lisburne Group. shale and phosphorite unit; sample from ~735.5 m above base of composite section.	Chandler Lake B-4 68°17.735', 151°54.869'.	Facies 6 Sample from an interval of two 10-cm-thick beds of calcareous phosphorite. Lower bed does not coarsen upward and consists of fine-sand-size phosphatic ooids and peloids with a few nodules as large as 2 cm in diameter. Upper bed coarsens upward from sand-size grains to nodules. Both beds have a calcareous and siliceous matrix with fluorite on fracture surfaces. Thin section is fine- to medium-grained phosphatic clasts (a few contain pyritized radiolarians?). minor silica cement, and trace purple fluorite. Sequence 5. HST	1 mid Pa element fragment of *Rhachistognathus prolixus* Baesemann and Lane 2 indet. bar and blade fragments	middle Late Mississippian (very early Chesterian). Upper age limit restricted by overlapping age range of conodont species in succeeding sample (field No. SKA 88.3).	~2.0	Indeterminate (too few conodonts).	Section SKB is a well-exposed interval of the phosphorite and black shale unit that is equivalent to the much more poorly exposed interval ~20-50 m above base of section SKA. Section SKB (32 m thick) is on strike with section SKA, in cliffs ~100-200 ft above streambed on east side of Skimo Creek. Heavy-mineral concentrate is chiefly phosphatized peloids and very fine grained rock fragments with scarce pale-purple fluorite fragments. 6.54 kg of rock was processed.
SKA 88.3 (33746-PC) Lisburne Group. lime mudstone unit; sample from ~775 m above base of composite section.	Chandler Lake B-4 68°17.766', 151°55.179'.	Facies 7 Sample from a 10-cm-thick bed of medium-dark-gray to medium-gray limestone that weathers light gray. Abundant brachiopods noted on bedding surface, but much of interval appears fine grained (muddy?). Thin section is skeletal mudstone-wackestone with peloids; bioclasts are brachiopods, crinoids, and rare bryozoans and ostracodes. Sequence 5. HST	This sample is the biostratigraphic golden spike that positions the section. 4 incomplete Pa elements *Cavusgnathus regularis* Youngquist and Miller 2 incomplete Pa elements *Cavusgnathus unicornis* Youngquist and Miller 7 Pa fragments *Cavusgnathus* spp. indet. 38 juvenile and subadult Pa elements *Gnathodus girtyi rhodesi* Higgins 3 Pa elements (1 juvenile, 1 subadult, and 1 adult) *Gnathodus texanus* Roundy 5 gnathodid M elements 51 juvenile and subadult Pa elements *Rhachistognathus prolixus* Baesemann and Lane Unassigned elements: 3 Pb (2 morphotypes), 3 Sa (2 morphotypes), 3 M, and 2 Sc 202 indet. bar, blade, and platform fragments	middle Late Mississippian (very early Chesterian). Occurrence of *Gnathodus texanus* with *Gn. girtyi rhodesi* and *Rhachistognathus prolixus* nicely restricts age of sample. Only one other collection from northern Alaska contains *Gn. texanus* with *Gn. girtyi simplex* or *Gn. girtyi rhodesi*—a sample from the Katakturuk River gorge section in the western Sadlerochit Mountains. NE. Brooks Range.	1.5	Conodonts represent a postmortem winnow from a rhachistognathid-gnathodid biofacies. Conodonts indicate a winnow because most are relatively small fragments or nearly complete to complete juveniles and subadults. Species association and its preservation suggest a relatively nearby. normal-marine. likely shoal water facies.	Heavy-mineral concentrate contains phosphatic brachiopod fragments, phosphatized ostracode and gastropod steinkerns, and rare pale purple amorphous fluorite and fluorite-replaced ichthyoliths. 6.4 kg of rock was processed.

Table 2. Conodont samples from the Skimo Creek section, northern Alaska.—Continued

[See figure 2 for locations. All samples collected by J.A. Dumoulin unless otherwise indicated; all faunas identified by A.G. Harris. CAI, conodont color-alteration index; indet., indeterminate; no., number]

Field No., (USGS colln. no.), stratigraphic unit, and position	Quadrangle, latitude N., longitude W.	Facies (table 1), lithology, and sequence position	Conodont fauna	Age	CAI	Conodont biofacies and depositional environment	Remarks
SKA 138.2 (34021-PC) Lisburne Group, lime mudstone unit; sample from ~825 m above base of composite section.	Chandler Lake B-4 68°17.812', 151°55.017'	Facies 1A Brownish-gray, skeletal-peloidal supportstone; sample from upper half of a 30-cm-thick bed at top of a 3-m-thick interval that coarsens upward from lime mudstone. Thin section is fine-grained skeletal-peloidal packstone–grainstone with outsized crinoid fragments, as large as 1 mm in diameter, and a large (0.5 cm diam) micritic intraclast; bioclasts include ostracodes (some articulated), bryozoan and coral(?) fragments, and calcispheres. Some bioclasts are bored, and a few have phosphatic coatings. Sequence 5. HST	50 mostly incomplete to complete Pa elements *Cavusgnathus* spp., including large specimens of *Cavusgnathus unicornis* Youngquist and Miller and C. *regularis* Youngquist and Miller 4 juvenile Pa elements *Gnathodus* spp. indet. of Late Mississippian morphotype *Kladognathus* sp. 1 M, 1 Sa fragment, 7 Sb-Sc element fragments, and 8 robust bar fragments Unassigned elements: 9 Pb (5 morphotypes), 7 M (5 morphotypes), and 2 Sb (2 morphotypes) 335 indet. bar, blade, and platform fragments	late Late Mississippian (Chesterian); lower age limit constrained by age of underlying collections.	2.0–2.5?	Cavusgnathid biofacies; abundance of conodont fragments and dominance of Pa elements of *Cavusgnathus* suggest derivation from a relatively high-energy, shallow-water depositional setting.	Heavy-mineral concentrate is made up almost entirely of phosphatic and phosphatized bioclasts, with very rare glauconite; bioclasts include, in order of decreasing abundance, conodonts, phosphatic brachiopod fragments, phosphatized bryozoan fragments, ichthyoliths, and rare small phosphatized gastropod steinkerns. 6.0 kg of rock was processed.
SKA 178C (33747-PC) Lisburne Group, lime mudstone unit; sample from ~865 m above base of composite section.	Chandler Lake B-4 Close to 68°17.84', 151°55.07'	Facies 1A Medium-gray limestone that weathers brownish gray, with 10–20 percent irregularly distributed nodules of dark-gray chert that we thin white to light brown. Skeletal packstone–wackestone with centimeter-thick grainy layers, crinoid ossicles (max 1 cm diam), productid brachiopods (max 10 cm diam), and locally abundant bryozoans. Thin section is crinoidal packstone–wackestone with lesser brachiopod and bryozoan fragments and abundant diagenetic quartz and dolomite. Sequence 5. HST	4 Pa elements *Cavusgnathus unicornis* Youngquist and Miller *Kladognathus* sp. indet. 1 Sa and 1 Sb-Sc element fragments 2 unassigned M elements 22 indet. bar, blade, and platform fragments Most conodonts are coated with organic matter and some are invaded by it (in the interlamellar space between apatite lamellae) so that the CAI value appears higher than is real. Two to three robust fragments that have no encrusting or invading organic matter clearly have a CAI value of 1.5.	late Late Mississippian (Chesterian); lower age limit constrained by age of underlying collections.	1.5	Indeterminate (too few conodonts). Likely postmortem transport from or within a shallow-water depositional setting.	Heavy-mineral concentrate contains bioclasts (mainly dolomitized bryozoan fragments and ichthyoliths), glauconite, and composite small pyrite clusters. 6.4 kg of rock was processed.

Table 2. Conodont samples from the Skimo Creek section, northern Alaska.—Continued

[See figure 2 for locations. All samples collected by J.A. Dumoulin unless otherwise indicated; all faunas identified by A.G. Harris. CAI, conodont color-alteration index; indet, indeterminate; no., number]

Field No., (USGS colln. no.), stratigraphic unit, and position	Quadrangle, latitude N., longitude W.	Facies (table 1), lithology, and sequence position	Conodont fauna	Age	CAI	Conodont biofacies and depositional environment	Remarks
SKA 187.1 (33748-PC) Lisburne Group, shale and spiculite unit; sample from ~874 m above base of composite section.	Chandler Lake B-4 Close to 68°17.84', 151°55.07'	Facies 8 Sample from upper 10 cm of a 45-cm-thick interval that is a probable omission surface. Greenish-weathering, greenish-gray glauconitic grainstone with irregular vertical burrows as large as 1 cm in diameter; forms platy beds, 1 to 2 cm thick. Lower 35 cm of interval is fine-grained, pyritic, glauconitic, supportstone to siltstone with productid brachiopods. Thin section is skeletal grainstone with notable phosphatic bioclasts and glauconite and lesser detrital quartz; several mud-filled burrows. Bioclasts (some bored) include brachiopod, crinoid, and ostracode fragments. Sequence 6	33 mostly incomplete and commonly abraded Pa elements *Gnathodus bilineatus* (Roundy) and (or) *Gn. bollandensis* (Higgins and Bouckaert) 2 Pa elements *Gnathodus simplex* Dunn 152 indet. bar, blade, and platform fragments Organic matter varyingly coats conodont elements, and lesser fine glauconite grains adhere to conodont surfaces.	late Late Mississippian (Chesterian, but not very earliest Chesterian). Age cannot be well restricted because both *Gn. girtyi simplex* and *Gn. bilineatus* are long-ranging in the Chesterian and preservation of *Gn. bilineatus* and (or) *Gn. bollandensis* does not allow definitive assignment of any specimens to *Gn. bollandensis*.	1.5	Gnathodid biofacies; drowned lag concentrate.	Heavy-mineral concentrate is chiefly pyritic, glauconitic, phosphatized carbonate rock fragments, with minor phosphatic brachiopod fragments, phosphatized pelmatozoan ossicles, and fluorite crystals. 6.6 kg of rock was processed.
SKA 202 Lisburne Group, shale and spiculite unit; sample from ~889 m above base of composite section.	Chandler Lake B-4 Very close to 68°17.84', 151°55.07'	Facies 5 Sample from a 50-cm-thick resistant lime mudstone interval inter-calated with recessive calcareous shale. Sample is sooty, grayish-black to black lime mudstone that weathers yellowish gray in platy, irregular beds, 2-6 cm thick, with scattered small brachiopods. Thin section is silty lime mudstone with brachiopod fragments, calcareous spicules, and minor quartz silt. Sequence 6	No conodonts were found.				Heavy-mineral concentrate includes scarce phosphatic brachiopod fragments. 6.4 kg of rock was processed.
SKA 210.5 (34022-PC) Lisburne Group, shale and spiculite unit; sample from ~897.5 m above base of composite section.	Chandler Lake B-4 Very close to 68°17.84', 151°55.07'	Facies 9 Sample from a 5- to 10-cm-thick, irregular bed of brownish-black, silty lime mudstone to limy siltstone with rare brachiopod(?) molds and pyrite-filled burrows. Thin section is mudstone with 20-30 percent dolomite rhombs, minor quartz silt, and thin lenses of calcareous spiculite with glauconite and phosphatic clasts. Sequence 6	1 incomplete unassigned Pb element 2 indet. conodont fragments	Conodonts in overlying and underlying samples constrain age to late Late Mississippian-Early Pennsylvanian (Chesterian-early Morrowan).	~1.5	Indeterminate.	6.0 kg of rock was processed.

Table 2. Conodont samples from the Skimo Creek section, northern Alaska.—Continued

[See figure 2 for locations. All samples collected by J.A. Dumoulin unless otherwise indicated; all faunas identified by A.G. Harris. CAI, conodont color-alteration index; indet., indeterminate; no., number]

Field No. (USGS colln. no.), stratigraphic unit, and position	Quadrangle, latitude N., longitude W.	Facies (table 1), lithology, and sequence position	Conodont fauna	Age	CAI	Conodont biofacies and depositional environment	Remarks
SKA 216.6 Lisburne Group, shale and spiculite unit; sample from ~903.6 m above base of composite section.	Chandler Lake B-4 68°17.84′, 151°55.07′	Facies 9 Sample from an ~50-cm-thick interval of medium-dark-gray spiculitic lime mudstone that weathers brownish gray and contains rare brachiopods, as large as 2 cm in diameter; overlain and underlain by noncalcareous, red-brown-weathering, dark-gray, locally silty shale. Thin section is silty lime mudstone with calcareous spicules and minor quartz silt and dolomite. Sequence 6	No conodonts were found.				Heavy-mineral concentrate contains rare pyrite and marcasite clusters and very rare phosphatic brachiopod fragments. 6.4 kg of rock was processed.
SKA 219 (33819-PC) Lisburne Group, shale and spiculite unit; sample from ~906 m above base of composite section.	Chandler Lake B-4 Close to but slightly south of 68°17.864′, 151°54.952′	Facies 9 Sample from a 5- to 15-cm-thick resistant interval that consists of thin (millimeter to centimeter thick) lenses of white limy siltstone (with crinoid ossicles, spines, glauconite, and pyrite) in dark shale. Limy siltstone preferentially sampled. Thin section is bioturbated mix of calcareous and siliceous sponge spicules in a matrix of noncarbonate mud and calcite cement; contains 10-20 percent quartz silt and fine sand, minor dolomite, glauconite, phosphatic clasts, barite, and pyrite, and rare ostracodes and crinoid ossicles. Sequence 6	1 Pa element fragment *Idioprioniodus* sp. indet. 49 Pa elements (mostly juveniles to subadults) of an intergradational population that ranges predominantly from specimens most like *Idiognathoides sinuatus* Harris and Hollingsworth to lesser numbers of specimens that could be assigned to *Declinognathodus noduliferous* (Ellison and Graves) 263 indet. bar, blade, and platform fragments	Early Pennsylvanian (early Morrowan); upper age limit constrained by conodonts in overlying sample (field No. SKA 221).	1.5-2.0	Postmortem transport within or from an *Idiognathoides* biofacies. Conodonts and mineralogy (presence of glauconite and glauconite-replaced small spicules) suggest relatively slow deposition.	Sample from 2 m below base of bright yellow soil that marks base of the Siksikpuk Formation here. Heavy-mineral concentrate contains abundant varyingly pyritic carbonate grains; lesser gray, slightly glauconitic and pyritic, silty to sandy grains; slightly tapering pyritized rods (likely pyritized sponge spicules); and scarce amorphous pyrite grains. 4.4 kg of rock was processed.

Table 2. Conodont samples from the Skimo Creek section, northern Alaska.—Continued

[See figure 2 for locations. All samples collected by J.A. Dumoulin unless otherwise indicated; all faunas identified by A.G. Harris. CAI, conodont color-alteration index; indet., indeterminate; no., number]

Field No., (USGS colln. no.), stratigraphic unit, and position	Quadrangle, latitude N., longitude W.	Facies (table 1), lithology, and sequence position	Conodont fauna	Age	CAI	Conodont biofacies and depositional environment	Remarks
SKA 221 (34023-PC) Lisburne Group. shale and spiculite unit; sample from highest exposed part of the Lisburne. ~908 m above base of composite section.	Chandler Lake B-4 Close to but slightly south of 68°17.864', 151°54.952'	Facies 9 Sample from a 10-cm-thick resistant bed of dark-gray to brownish-black, rusty-brown-weathering, locally graded, calcareous, siliceous, and pyritic spiculite with disseminated glauconite and phosphate, local burrows, and wispy laminae. Thin section is bioturbated mix of noncarbonate mud and calcareous spiculite, with silt- to sand-size quartz, phosphate, and glauconite. Sequence 6	35 Pa elements *Declinognathodus noduliferus* (Ellison and Graves) 36 Pa elements *Idiognathoides sinuatus* Harris and Hollingsworth 8 Pa elements *Rhachistognathus websteri* Baesemann and Lane Unassigned elements: 7 Pb (3 morphotypes), 1 M, and 3 Sc 484 indet. bar, blade, and platform fragments	Early Pennsylvanian (early Morrowan). *Idiognathoides sinuatus* first appears in the early Pennsylvanian, and *Rh. websteri* does not occur above the *I. sinuatus* Zone of the early Morrowan.	1.5–2.0	This is a normal-marine species association; *Rh. websteri*, a shallow-water species, was probably a post-mortem hydraulic addition.	Sampled bed immediately overlain by yellow-weathering beds of the basal Siksikpuk Formation. Heavy-mineral concentrate consists chiefly of composite grains of pyrite and glauconite, lesser phosphatic grains, and rare coniform ichthyoliths. 6.0 kg of rock was processed.
SKA 230 (33776-PC) Siksikpuk Formation; sample from limestone bed that forms top of unit A, ~9 m above base of formation and 917 m above base of composite section.	Chandler Lake B-4 68°17.864', 151°54.952'	Sample from near top of a 2- to 3-m-thick interval of very light gray to light-olive-gray (weathered and fresh), fine-grained limestone in blocky to slightly irregular beds 3–4 cm thick; contains brachiopods, gastropods, and bivalves(?). Thin section is fine-grained argillaceous limestone with rare bioclasts (mainly bryozoan, brachiopod, and crinoid fragments) and phosphatic grains.	6 waterworn Pa element fragments of a streptognathodid and (or) idiognathodid 1 Pb element 33 indet. conodont fragments	Likely Early Permian.	~3.0	Indeterminate (too few and poorly preserved conodonts).	Brachiopods from this bed identified as early Early Permian (Wolfcampian) by J.T. Dutro (in Siok, 1985). Heavy-mineral concentrate contains euhedral and amorphous pyrite grains, white dolomitic steinkerns (8 gastropod and 6 smooth-shelled ostracode), 1 ichthyolith, and 1 phosphatized bryozoan fragment. 6.75 kg of rock was processed.

Table 3.   Conodont samples from the Tiglukpuk Creek section, northern Alaska.

[See figure 2 for locations. All samples collected by J.A. Dumoulin; all faunas identified by A.G. Harris. CAI, conodont color-alteration index; indet., indeterminate; no., number]

Field No. (USGS colln. no.), stratigraphic unit, and position	Quadrangle, latitude N., longitude W.	Facies (table 1), lithology, and sequence position	Conodont fauna	Age	CAI	Conodont biofacies and depositional environment	Remarks
TNA 1 (33674-PC) Lisburne Group, nodular limestone and dolostone unit; sample from 1 m above base of section, which represents lowest exposure of the Lisburne Group on south limb of the Tiglukpuk anticline.	Chandler Lake B-4 68°22.523', 151°52.689'	Facies 1B Medium-brownish-gray limestone that weathers grayish orange. Fetid crinoidal grainstone in 30- to 50-cm-thick beds; near middle of 2.8-m-thick coarsening upward interval. Thin section is crinoidal grainstone with minor disarticulated ostracode valves and brachiopod fragments (max 1 cm long); sample has open packing, and partial silicification of some bioclasts. Sequence 2, TST	1 Pa element posterior fragment *Bispathodus utahensis* Sandberg and Gutschick or *Hindeodus* aff. *Hi. crassidentatus* (Branson and Mehl) 3 Sb-Sc element fragments *Kladognathus* sp. 20 indet. bar, blade, and platform fragments	late Early Mississippian (late Kinderhookian-Osagean); *Polygnathus communis* in overlying sample TNA 43 restricts upper age limit to Osagean.	1.5–2.0	Indeterminate (too few conodonts); conodonts present indicate postmortem transport from or within a relatively shallow-water depositional setting.	Section in west-central part of sec. 27, T. 12 S., R. 1 E., on east side of Tiglukpuk Creek, elevation ~2,100 ft. Heavy-mineral concentrate is chiefly phosphatized bioclasts including, in order of decreasing abundance, fragments and steinkerns of phosphatized bryozoans (including fenestrate forms), coralline fragments, diverse ichthyoliths, gastropod steinkerns, and phosphatic brachiopod fragments. 10.1 kg of rock was processed.
TNA 43 (33675-PC) Lisburne Group, nodular limestone and dolostone unit; sample from 43 m above base of section.	Chandler Lake B-4 68°22.468', 151°52.707'	Facies 1A Brownish-gray limestone that weathers medium gray to grayish orange. Fetid, fine- to medium-grained crinoidal supportstone in 10- to 20-cm-thick beds near middle of 2-m-thick interval (local specks of dead oil?). Thin section is crinoidal packstone-grainstone with bryozoan and trilobite(?) fragments, and minor dolomite and silica replacement. Sequence 2, HST	*Hindeodus* aff. *Hi. crassidentatus* (Branson and Mehl) 25 Pa (all incomplete) and 3 Pb elements *Kladognathus* sp. 6 M and 5 Sb-Sc element fragments 5 Pa element fragments *Polygnathus communis* (Branson and Mehl) *Synclydognathus geminus* (Hinde) 20 Pa mostly incomplete posterior fragments and 2 Sb elements Unassigned elements: 4 M (3 morphotypes) 110 indet. bar, blade, and platform fragments	late Early Mississippian (Osagean).	1.5–2.0	Hindeodid-synclydognathid biofacies; relatively shallow water depositional setting.	6.1 kg of rock was processed.
TNA 94.5 (33676-PC) Lisburne Group, nodular limestone and dolostone unit; sample from 94.5 m above base of section.	Chandler Lake B-4 68°22.421', 151°52.740'	Facies 1A Brownish-gray limestone that weathers pale orange to pale yellowish brown. Fetid crinoidal supportstone (some ossicles as large as 5 mm diam) in decimeter-thick beds; top of 1-m-thick cycle grading upward from wackestone to packstone-grainstone. Thin section is crinoidal grainstone with notable ostracode valves (some articulated), open packing, and traces of dolomite and silica. Sequence 2, HST	3 incomplete Pa elements *Bispathodus utahensis* Sandberg and Gutschick 1 Pa element *Hindeodus* aff. *Hi. crassidentatus* (Branson and Mehl) *Kladognathus* sp. 1 M, 1 Sa, and 2 Sb-Sc element fragments Unassigned elements: 1 Pb and 1 M 8 indet. bar, blade, and platform fragments	late Early Mississippian (Osagean); age range constrained by presence of *Polygnathus communis* in TNA 43.	1.5–2.0	Indeterminate (too few conodonts); conodonts present indicate postmortem transport within or from a shallow-water depositional setting.	Heavy-mineral concentrate contains phosphatic clasts and bioclasts (including phosphatic brachiopods, phosphatized bryozoan colonies, ostracode valves and steinkerns, and scarce gastropods and ichthyoliths). 6.2 kg of rock was processed.

Table 3. Conodont samples from the Tiglukpuk Creek section, northern Alaska.—Continued

[See figure 2 for locations. All samples collected by J.A. Dumoulin; all faunas identified by A.G. Harris. CAI, conodont color-alteration index; indet., indeterminate; no., number]

Field No., (USGS colln. no.), stratigraphic unit, and position	Quadrangle, latitude N., longitude W.	Facies (table 1), lithology, and sequence position	Conodont fauna	Age	CAI	Conodont biofacies and depositional environment	Remarks
TNB 45.5 (34019-PC) Lisburne Group, nodular limestone and dolostone unit; sample from ~154 m above base of composite section.	Chandler Lake B-4; 68°22.375'; 151°52.627'.	Facies 1B. Crossbedded, light-brownish-gray to white limestone (crinoid grainstone), locally dolomitized, with abundant dead oil; from 5-cm-thick interval with 0.5- to 1-m-thick beds. Thin section is completely dolomitized crinoidal grainstone with notable intercrystalline dead oil. Sequence 2. HST	9 small, unassigned conodont fragments	Mississippian, based on stratigraphic position.	1.5–2.0	Few, small, and taxonomically indeterminate conodont fragments are postmortem additions; the environment from which they were derived is indeterminate.	Section TNB begins at or very close to top of section TNA and extends from west-central to southwestern part of sec. 27, T. 12 S., R. 1 E., on east side of Tiglukpuk Creek. Heavy-mineral concentrate includes rare to scarce phosphatized bryozoan fragments and conical fish teeth. 6.0 kg of rock was processed.
TNB 63 (33677-PC) Lisburne Group, nodular limestone and dolostone unit; sample from ~171 m above base of composite section.	Chandler Lake B-4; 68°22.319'; 151°52.773'.	Facies 1A. Sample from 20-cm-thick lens of grayish-orange-weathering, light-brownish-gray, medium-grained crinoidal packstone grainstone with abundant smooth-shelled ostracodes. Thin section is foraminiferal grainstone packstone with disarticulated ostracode valves, crinoid fragments, and peloids. Sequence 3. TST	*Cloghergnathus* sp. transitional to *Cavusgnathus unicornis* Youngquist and Miller. 6 Pa and 1 Sc elements (all fractured or incomplete). *Hindeodus* aff. *Hi. crassidentatus* (Branson and Mehl) transitional to *Hi. cristulus* (Youngquist and Miller). 31 Pa and 3 Pb elements. 23 indet. bar, blade, and platform fragments	latest Early–very earliest Late Mississippian (very late Osagean–early late Meramecian); age constrained by *Polygnathus mehli* in collection TNB 134.5. *Cloghergnathus* sp. is typical of shallow water settings with fluctuating, commonly elevated salinities.	1.5–2.0	Postmortem transport within or from hindeodid biofacies; relatively shallow water, likely normal marine depositional setting.	Heavy-mineral concentrate is chiefly bioclasts (mainly dolomitized and phosphatized bryozoans, corals, and lesser pelmatozoans, phosphatic brachiopods, and ichthyoliths) and includes rare fluorite. 6.9 kg of rock was processed.
TNB 134.5 (33678-PC) Lisburne Group, nodular limestone and dolostone unit; sample from ~243 m above base of composite section.	Chandler Lake B-4; 68°22.279'; 151°52.695'.	Facies 1A. Sample from 30-cm-thick lens (2-3 m wide) of crinoidal packstone grainstone in 10- to 15-cm-thick beds, in 3-4-m-thick interval of thin-bedded cherty wackestone. Sample is light-brownish-gray, fetid dolomitic limestone that weathers light gray. Thin section is crinoidal grainstone with open packing; other bioclasts include ostracode valves (some articulated), foraminifers, and bryozoan and brachiopod fragments. Sequence 3. HST	2 Pa elements *Cavusgnathus unicornis* Youngquist and Miller or a transition form from *Cloghergnathus* sp. 6 Pa elements (all incomplete) *Hindeodus* aff. *Hi. crassidentatus* (Branson and Mehl) *Kladognathus* sp. 4 M, 3 Sa, 7 Sb-Sc elements and 2 long bar fragments. 1 incomplete Pa element *Polygnathus mehli* Thompson. 13 indet. bar, blade, and platform fragments	latest Early–very earliest Late Mississippian (very late Osagean–very early late Meramecian), based on occurrence of possible *Cloghergnathus* stratigraphically below (TNB 63) and in this collection with *Polygnathus mehli*.	1.5–2.0	Postmortem transport within or from a shallow-water, relatively normal marine setting.	Heavy-mineral concentrate includes rare glauconite and abundant dolomitized, phosphatized, and phosphatic bioclasts; bioclasts (in order of decreasing abundance) are bryozoan-colony fragments, gastropod steinkerns, and ichthyoliths. 6.0 kg of rock was processed.

Table 3. Conodont samples from the Tiglukpuk Creek section, northern Alaska.—Continued

[See figure 2 for locations. All samples collected by J.A. Dumoulin; all faunas identified by A.G. Harris. CAI, conodont color-alteration index; indet., indeterminate; no., number]

Field No., (USGS colln. no.), stratigraphic unit, and position	Quadrangle, latitude N., longitude W.	Facies (table 1), lithology, and sequence position	Conodont fauna	Age	CAI	Conodont biofacies and depositional environment	Remarks
TNB 206.2 (33679-PC) Lisburne Group, nodular limestone and dolostone unit; sample from ~314 m above base of composite section.	Chandler Lake B-4 68°22.196', 151°52.705'	Facies 1B. Brownish-gray limestone (locally dolomitic) that weathers light- to medium-ligh -gray. Very fetid, diverse skele al supportstone; in 10- to 15-cm-thick beds; bioclasts (max 1 cm diam) include crinoids, smooth pentamerid and ribbed spriferid brachiopods, and trilobite and fenestrale bryozoan fragments. Local intergranular dead oil. Upper part of 1-m-thick cycle grading upward from wackestone-packstone to packstone-grainstone. Thin section is dolomitized crinoidal grainstone w th patchy dead oil and minor glauconite. Sequence 3. HST.	*Bispathodus utahensis* Sandberg and Gutschick 32 Pa (mostly incomplete), 2 Pb, and 4 M elements. 5 Pa elements *Cavusgnathus unicornis* Youngquist and Miller or a transitional form from *Cloghergnathus* sp. *Kladognathus* sp. 5 M and 8 Sb-Sc elements. 1 Pa element *Synchydognathus geminus* (Hinde). Unassigned elements: 2 Pb (2 morphotypes), 5 Sa (2 morphotypes), and 6 Sc (2 morphotypes) 320 indet. bar, blade, and platform fragments	early Late Mississippian (Meramecian, probably early Meramecian).	1.5	Postmortem transport within or from bispathodid biofacies. Abundance of relatively small conodont fragments indicates a postmortem winnow, and faunal composition suggests a shallow- or near-shallow-water depositional regime.	Heavy-mineral concentrate is chiefly bioclasts (including phosphatized colonial coral and bryozoan fragments and phosphatic brachiopods); some carbonate grains and bioclasts in residue are coated with dead oil. 7.4 kg of rock was processed.
TNB 264.4 (33680-PC) Lisburne Group, lower packstone and grainstone unit; sample from ~373 m above base of composite section.	Chandler Lake B-4 68°22.145', 151°52.682'	Facies 1A. Very light- to light-gray-weathering, light-brownish-gray, fetid grainstone in blocky, even beds (30 to 40 cm thick); some crinoid ossicles are as large as 4 mm in diameter. Thin section is coarse-grained crinoidal grainstone. Sequence 4, TST.	2 Pa elements *Bispathodus utahensis* Sandberg and Gutschick *Cavusgnathus unicornis* Youngquist and Miller or a transitional form from *Cloghergnathus* sp. 7 incomplete Pa and 1 Pb elements subadult Pa element *Cloghergnathus carinatus* Higgins and Varker (anterior blade missing) has nodose margins and carina, as in much of the topotype material, and more of the characteristics of *Cloghergnathus* than the other specimens Pa element *Hindeodus cristulus* (Youngquist and Miller)? *Kladognathus* sp. 10 M, 5 Sa, and 4 Sb-Sc incomplete elements 26 indet. bar, blade, and platform fragments	early Late Mississippian (Meramecian, probably early Meramecian).	1.5	Postmortem transport within a high-energy, shallow-water depositional setting.	Heavy-mineral concentrate contains abundant phosphatic, phosphatized, and dolomitized bioclasts, including phosphatized bryozoans, phosphatic brachiopods, and ichthyoliths. 8.5 kg of rock was processed.

Table 3.   Conodont samples from the Tiglukpuk Creek section, northern Alaska.—Continued

[See figure 2 for locations. All samples collected by J.A. Dumoulin; all faunas identified by A.G. Harris. CAI, conodont color-alteration index; indet., indeterminate; no., number]

Field No., (USGS colln. no.), stratigraphic unit, and position	Quadrangle, latitude N., longitude W.	Facies (table 1), lithology, and sequence position	Conodont fauna	Age	CAI	Conodont biofacies and depositional environment	Remarks
TNC 1.6 (33777-PC) Lisburne Group, lower packstone and grainstone unit; sample from ~457 m above base of composite section.	Chandler Lake B-4 68°22.093', 151°52.542'	Facies 1(A?) Sample from 20 cm above base of a 1.3-m-thick interval of plane laminated, light-gray-weathering, medium-gray limestone (crinoidal grainstone) in 10- to 30-cm-thick beds. Thin section is skeletal packstone-grainstone; clasts are crinoid, bryozoan, and brachiopod fragments, diverse foraminifers, ostracode valves (some articulated), and minor peloids. Sequence 4, TST	4 Pa elements *Cavusgnathus regularis* Youngquist and Miller 2 Pa element fragments *Cavusgnathus* sp. 2 Sc element fragments *Kladognathus* sp. Unassigned elements: 3 incomplete M (3 morphotypes) 19 indet. bar, blade, and platform fragments	middle Late Mississippian (late Meramecian-very early Chesterian); upper age limit constrained by overlying sample.	2.0	Biofacies indeterminate (too few conodonts); conodont species association and condition denote a relatively high energy regime because only the most robust elements (Pa elements of *Cavusgnathus*, robust fragments of *Cavusgnathus* and *Kladognathus*) are nearly complete.	Section TNC is separated from the top of section TNB by 25.3 m of cover; it begins on the south-central edge of sec. 27, T. 12 S., R. 1 E. Heavy-mineral concentrate includes minor pelmatozoan ossicles and columnals. 6.0 kg of rock was processed.
TNC 69.5 (33778-PC) Lisburne Group, lower packstone and grainstone unit; sample from ~525 m above base of composite section.	Chandler Lake B-4 68°21.988', 151°52.494'	Facies 1B Sample from 2 m above base of a 2.7-m-thick interval of cross-laminated(?), dark-grayish-brown-weathering, light-grayish-brown limestone (crinoidal supportstone with solitary rugose corals) in 2- to 15-cm-thick beds. Thin section is overpacked crinoidal packstone with varied bryozoan fragments, an articulated brachiopod, rare foraminifers, numerous stylolites, and minor dead oil. Sequence 4, HST	4 incomplete Pa elements *Cavusgnathus* sp. indet. 1 S element fragment *Synclydognathus* sp. indet. 1 unassigned Pb element 29 indet. bar, blade, and platform fragments	middle Late Mississippian (late Meramecian-very early Chesterian).	1.5-2.0	Biofacies indeterminate (too few conodonts); conodonts present indicate a relatively shallow water, high-energy depositional setting.	6.0 kg of rock was processed.

Table 3.   Conodont samples from the Tiglukpuk Creek section, northern Alaska.—Continued

[See figure 2 for locations. All samples collected by J.A. Dumoulin; all faunas identified by A.G. Harris. CAI, conodont color-alteration index; indet., indeterminate; no., number]

Field No., (USGS colln. no.), stratigraphic unit, and position	Quadrangle, latitude N., longitude W.	Facies (table 1), lithology, and sequence position	Conodont fauna	Age	CAI	Conodont biofacies and depositional environment	Remarks
TNC 152 (33779-PC) Lisburne Group, lower packstone and grainstone unit; sample from ~607 m above base of composite section.	Chandler Lake B-4 Close to (but slightly north of) 68°21.877', 151°52.487'	Facies 1B Sample from ~5 m above base of a 17.4-m-thick interval of light-brown-weathering, light-gray limestone (fine-grained crinoidal grainstone) in 10- to 70-cm-thick beds with local parallel (and cross?) lamination. Sample from near top of ~70-cm-thick bed. Thin section is fine-grained crinoidal-bryozoan grainstone with minor dolomite and a few patches of possible dead oil. Sequence 4. HST	24 incomplete to complete Pa and 3 Pb elements *Cavusgnathus regularis* Youngquist and Miller 4 incomplete Pa elements *Hindeodus* spp. 5 Pa *Hindeodus* aff. *Hi. crassidentatus* Branson and Mehl *Kladognathus* sp. 39 P, 3 M, 3 Sa, and 33 Sb-Sc mostly incomplete elements *Lochriea commutata* (Branson and Mehl) 2 Pa and 3 M elements *Synclydognathus geminus* (Hinde) 6 Pa, 1 M, and 7 S elements Unassigned elements: 4 Pa, 24 M (4 morphotypes), and 4 Sc 664 indet. bar, blade, and platform fragments	middle Late Mississippian (late Meramecian–very early Chesterian; Lower *Cavusgnathus* Zone into lower part of *Gnathodus bilineatus*-Upper *Cavusgnathus* Zone).	1.5–2.0	Kladognathid-cavusgnathid biofacies. Abundance of small, incomplete fragments suggests a high-energy depositional setting. Most conodont species, with the possible exception of *Lochriea commutata*, are typical of nearshore settings.	Heavy-mineral concentrate contains phosphatic brachiopod fragments, rare ichthyoliths, and scarce purple fluorite. 6.0 kg of rock was processed.
TNC 197 (34020-PC) Lisburne Group, chert and phosphorite unit, sample from ~652 m above base of composite section.	Chandler Lake B-4 68°21.87', 151°52.44'	Facies 6 Nodular 3- to 8-cm-thick beds of medium-gray to light-brownish-gray crinoidal grainstone with black sand- to pebble-size phosphatic grains and thin muddy laminae. ~0.5 cm thick. Sample is ~4-5 m stratigraphically above level of abundant phosphorite rubble. Thin section is skeletal-peloidal grainstone with several phosphatic clasts and carbonate intraclasts; bioclasts include crinoid, bryozoan, ostracode, a nd brachiopod fragments, foraminifers, and algae. Many bioclasts are partially to completely micritized. Sequence 5. HST	17 Pa element fragments *Cavusgnathus* sp. indet. 1 Pa *Cavusgnathus regularis* Youngquist and Miller 3 Pa elements *Cavusgnathus unicornis* Youngquist and Miller 2 Pa elements *Gnathodus bilineatus* Roundy 220 Pa elements *Gnathodus girtyi girtyi* Hass 44 Pa elements *Gnathodus texanus* Roundy 13 *Idioprioniodus* sp. fragments *Kladognathus tenuis* 3 M, 3 Sa, and 5 Sc element fragments 179 complete to incomplete Pa elements *Rhachistognathus prolixus* Baesemann and Lane Unassigned elements: 2 Pb (2 morphotypes), 5 M (3 morphotypes), and 1 Sc fragment 1,988 indet. bar, blade, and platform fragments	middle Late Mississippian (early Chesterian; *Gn. bilineatus*-Upper *Cavusgnathus* Zone) on the basis of the overlapping ranges of *Gn. texanus* and *Rh. prolixus*.	1.5–2.0	Gnathodid-rhachistognathid biofacies, indicating normal-marine depositional setting and likely postmortem hydraulic transport farther seaward of lighter ramiform elements.	NW1/4 sec. 34, T. 12 S., R. 1 E., east side of Tiglukpuk Creek. Heavy-mineral concentrate is chiefly phosphatized (originally carbonate) rock fragments, subordinate phosphatized and phosphatic fossils. Bioclasts are, in order of decreasing abundance: crinoid ossicles and columnals, low-spired (abundant) and high-spired (scarce) gastropod steinkerns, pelecypod steinkerns, lesser ornate and smooth ostracode steinkerns, and minor phosphatized bryozoan fragments. 6.0 kg of rock was processed.

Table 3. Conodont samples from the Tiglukpuk Creek section, northern Alaska.—Continued

[See figure 2 for locations. All samples collected by J.A. Dumoulin; all faunas identified by A.G. Harris. CAI, conodont color-alteration index; indet., indeterminate; no., number]

Field No., (USGS colln. no.), stratigraphic unit, and position	Quadrangle, latitude N., longitude W.	Facies (table 1), lithology, and sequence position	Conodont fauna	Age	CAI	Conodont biofacies and depositional environment	Remarks
TND 2.3 (33780-PC) Lisburne Group, upper packstone and grainstone unit; sample from ~669 m above base of composite section.	Chandler Lake B-4 68°21.84', 151°52.57'	Facies 1 (B?) Sample from top of a 2.3-m-thick interval of medium-gray-weathering, medium-brownish-gray limestone (skeletal packstone-grainstone with crinoids, bryozoans, and brachiopods) in 30- to 40-cm-thick beds. Thin section is partially dolomitized bryozoan packstone with crinoid and brachiopod fragments and foraminifers. Sequence 5, HST	11 predominantly incomplete (1 complete juvenile) mostly juvenile Pa elements *Cavusgnathus* sp. indet. 5 incomplete elements of *Cavusgnathus* sp. and *Kladognathus* sp. *Kladognathus* sp. 1 Sa and 3 Sb-Sc element fragments 2 unassigned incomplete Sc elements 434 indet. bar, blade, and platform fragments	middle Late Mississippian (early Chesterian); age constrained by underlying and overlying samples.	1.5–2.0	Absence of complete conodont elements except for 1 juvenile Pa *Cavusgnathus* sp. and overwhelming abundance of small conodont fragments indicate postmortem transport from a high-energy environment.	Section TND begins close to the stratigraphic top of TNC but is on west side of stream (NW1/4 sec. 34). Heavy-mineral concentrate contains dolomitized and phosphatized colonial coral and bryozoan fragments. 6.0 kg of rock was processed.
TND 33.2 (33781-PC) Lisburne Group, upper packstone and grainstone unit; sample from ~700 m above base of composite section.	Chandler Lake B-4 Close to (but slightly south of) 68°21.84', 151°52.57'	Facies 1 (B?) Sample near top of 7.2-m-thick interval of gray-brown-weathering, medium-gray dolomitic(?) limestone in 5- to 30-cm-thick beds. Sample is skeletal supportstone with crinoids and bryozoans that forms lenses within muddier rocks. Thin section is mostly coarse-grained crinoidal grainstone with subordinate disseminated peloids, minor bryozoan and ostracode(?) fragments, and a layer of fine-grained skeletal-peloidal grainstone near top. Sequence 5, HST	42 Pa elements (chiefly juveniles) *Cavusgnathus regularis* Youngquist and Miller 1 M and 1 Sc elements *Cavusgnathus* sp. 20 juvenile Pa elements *Gnathodus* cf. *Gn. girtyi simplex* Dunn 2 juvenile Pa elements *Gnathodus texanus* Roundy 1 Pa element aff. *Lochriea commutata* (Branson and Mehl) 285 indet. bar, blade, and platform fragments	middle Late Mississippian (early Chesterian); age constrained by underlying sample.	1.5–2.0	Postmortem transport within or from a cavusgnathid-gnathodid biofacies.	Heavy-mineral concentrate contains phosphatized and phosphatic bioclasts (chiefly bryozoans and phosphatic brachiopod fragments) and minor pale-purple fluorite. 6.0 kg of rock was processed.

Table 3. Conodont samples from the Tiglukpuk Creek section, northern Alaska.—Continued

[See figure 2 for locations. All samples collected by J.A. Dumoulin; all faunas identified by A.G. Harris. CAI, conodont color-alteration index; indet., indeterminate; no., number]

Field No., (USGS colln. no.), stratigraphic unit, and position	Quadrangle, latitude N., longitude W.	Facies (table 1), lithology, and sequence position	Conodont fauna	Age	CAI	Conodont biofacies and depositional environment	Remarks
TN GPS 029 (33681-PC) Lisburne Group, upper packstone and grainstone unit; sample from ~720-725 m above base of composite section (1 m below top of highest major exposure of the Lisburne Group here).	Chandler Lake B-4 68°21.786'. 151°52.635'.	Facies 1 Fetid crinoidal packstone in blocky irregular beds, a few centimeters to 15 cm thick, with minor ovoids and layers of tan to black chert (some with concentric color banding). Thin section is bryozoan-crinoidal packstone with one articulated brachiopod. Sequence 5, HST	2 Pa elements (including 1 juvenile) *Cavusgnathus unicornis* Youngquist and Miller 7 juvenile Pa elements *Gnathodus* sp. 5 juvenile Pa elements *Vogelgnathus campbelli* (Rexroad) Unassigned elements: 1 Pb and 1 Sc 11 indet. bar, blade, and platform fragments	late Late Mississippian (Chesterian); age constrained by underlying sample.	1.5	Indeterminate (too few conodonts).	On east side of Tiglukpuk Creek, elevation, ~2,100 ft. NW1/4 sec. 34, T. 12 S., R. 1 E. 5.1 kg of rock was processed.
TN 95.9 (33673-PC) Lisburne Group, nodular limestone and dolostone unit; sample likely equivalent to a level ~148 m above base of composite section.	Chandler Lake B-4 68°22.759'. 151°52.486'.	Facies 1 Massive, brownish-gray limestone that weathers pale yellowish brown. Fetid crinoidal packstone with local rugose corals and abundant calcite veins. Thin section is partially dolomitized fine-grained crinoidal packstone, with one articulated ostracode, possible burrows, and seams of organic material. Sequence 2, HST	2 Pa element fragments *Bispathodus utahensis* Sandberg and Gutschick *Kladognathus* sp. indet. 1 M, 1 Sa, and 2 Sb-Sc tiny element fragments 3-4 indet. small bar, blade, and platform fragments	latest Early-very earliest Late Mississippian (very late Osagean-early Meramecian); age constrained by overlying collection (field No. TN 1.5).	1.5-2.0	Indeterminate (too few conodonts); conodonts present indicate postmortem transport from or within a relatively shallow water depositional setting.	Section TN was measured on north limb of Tiglukpuk anticline, likely equivalent to lower part of section TNB; north-central part of sec. 27, T. 12 S., R. 1 E. Section starts (TN 0) on north side of unnamed tributary to Tiglukpuk Creek, and continues southward along east side of Tiglukpuk Creek; elevation, ~2,100 ft. 10.2 kg of rock was processed.

Table 3.   Conodont samples from the Tiglukpuk Creek section, northern Alaska.—Continued

[See figure 2 for locations. All samples collected by J.A. Dumoulin; all faunas identified by A.G. Harris. CAI, conodont color-alteration index; indet., indeterminate; no., number]

Field No., (USGS colln. no.), stratigraphic unit, and position	Quadrangle, latitude N., longitude W.	Facies (table 1), lithology, and sequence position	Conodont fauna	Age	CAI	Conodont biofacies and depositional environment	Remarks
TN 19.3 (33672-PC) Lisburne Group, nodular limestone and dolostone unit; sample likely equivalent to a level ~223 m above base of composite section.	Chandler Lake B-4 68°22.780′, 151°52.321′	Facies 1A Medium-brownish-gray limestone with hints of pale red that weathers light gray to medium dark gray. Sample from 20-cm-thick bed of coarse-grained, diverse skeletal supportstone with abundant brachiopods, as well as crinoids, fenestrate bryozoans, and scaphipods(?). Thin section is crinoidal grainstone with varied bryozoan and brachiopod fragments, ostracodes (some articulated), and one spired gastropod. Sequence 3, HST	1 Pa element fragment *Bispathodus utahensis* Sandberg and Gutschick *Kladognathus* sp. indet. 1 incomplete Pa and 3 Sb-Sc element fragments 21 indet. bar, blade, and platform fragments	latest Early–very earliest Late Mississippian (very late Osagean–early Meramecian); age constrained by overlying sample.	1.5–2.0	Indeterminate (too few conodonts); conodonts present indicate postmortem transport from or within a relatively shallow water depositional setting.	Heavy-mineral concentrate is chiefly dolomitized pelmatozoan ossicles with minor phosphatic brachiopod fragments and scarce phosphatized gastropod steinkerns and ichthyoliths. 9.1 kg of rock was processed.
TN 1.5 (33671-PC) Lisburne Group, nodular limestone and dolostone unit; sample likely equivalent to a level ~240 m above base of composite section.	Chandler Lake B-4 68°22.788′, 151°52.367′	Facies 4? Brownish-black limestone that weathers pale yellow orange to light to medium light gray. Fetid skeletal wackestone in platy ≤2-cm-thick beds, with small pelmatozoan ossicles, rugose corals, and brachiopods; calcite veins locally abundant. Thin section is partially dolomitized skeletal wackestone-packstone; bioclasts include partially silicified crinoid ossicles, lesser ostracodes (some articulated), bryozoan fragments, foraminifers, and spired gastropods. Minor patches of possible dead oil. Sequence 3, HST	7 Pa element fragments *Cloghergnathus* sp. or *Cavusgnathus* sp. indet. 1 M element *Kladognathus* sp. indet. 1 Sc element *Synclydognathus geminus* (Hinde) 4 indet. fragments Purnell (1992) synonymized *Cloghergnathus* with *Taphrognathus* which is the senior taxon. For the time being, we are still using *Cloghergnathus* as a separate genus because it seems to be transitional between *Taphrognathus* and *Cavusgnathus*.	latest Early–very earliest Late Mississippian (very late Osagean–early Meramecian). *Cloghergnathus* sp. is typical of shallow-water settings with fluctuating, commonly elevated salinities.	1.5–2.0	Indeterminate (too few conodonts); conodonts present indicate postmortem transport from or within a relatively shallow water depositional setting.	Heavy-mineral concentrate contains blackened carbonate grains (coated with dead oil?) 9.5 kg of rock was processed.

Table 4.   Other conodont samples from the study area in northern Alaska.

[See figures 1 and 2 for locations. All samples collected by J.A. Dumoulin unless otherwise indicated; all faunas identified by A.G. Harris unless otherwise indicated. CAI, conodont color-alteration index; indet, indeterminate; no., number]

Map no., (field, USGS colln. nos.), stratigraphic unit, and position	Quadrangle, latitude N., longitude W.	Facies (table 1), lithology, and sequence position	Conodont fauna	Age	CAI	Conodont biofacies and depositional environment	Remarks
Skimo thrust sheet							
Loc. 4, fig. 2 (CC-1) Lisburne Group. lime mudstone unit; sample from ~40 m above 24-m-thick interval of black shale and phosphorite; likely equivalent to field No. SKA 88.3.	Chandler Lake B-4 68°17'32", 152°01'10" East side of Confusion Creek; north-central part of sec. 25, T. 13 S., R. 1 W.	Facies 1A Medium-dark-gray to dark-gray, very fetid limestone that weathers medium light gray; skeletal supportstone with crinoid ossicles (max >1 mm diam) and phosphatic pebbles (max 3.5 mm long). Thin section is closely packed skeletal grainstone with abundant phosphatic clasts and patchy phosphatic cement; bioclasts include crinoid, ostracode, gastropod, and brachiopod fragments. Sequence 5, HST.	*Cavusgnathus altus* Harris and Hollingsworth 6 Pa, 1 Pb elements 8 cavusgnathid Pa fragments 1 Pa *Gnathodus texanus* Roundy 2 P elements *Kladognathus* sp. indet. 59 Pa *Rhachistognathus prolixus* 21 Pa *Rhachistognathus* sp. indet. (juveniles and broken Pa fragments, probably *Rh. prolixus*) 2 indet elements *Idioprioniodus* sp. indet. Unassigned elements: 1 Pb, 4 M (2 morphotypes) 71 indet. bar, blade, and platform fragments	middle Late Mississippian (early Chesterian).	1.5-2.0	Postmortem transport within or from a rhachistognathid biofacies, which is a high-energy, near-shoal-water facies.	This fauna is similar to that from field No. SKA 88.3, from ~775 m above base of the Lisburne Group. Confusion Creek section is ~4.4 km west of Skimo Creek. Heavy-mineral concentrate consists mainly of oil-stained phosphatic clasts and bioclasts, including crinoids and ostracode and gastropod steinkerns. Lamellae in many conodont elements contain dead oil. 5.9 kg of rock was processed. Sample collected by Jeff Lukasic, Petro-Canada Oil & Gas. Collection identified by Andrea Krumhardt, University of Alaska, Fairbanks.
Loc. 4, fig. 2 (CC-0, 34028-PC) Lisburne Group. lime mudstone unit; sample equivalent to field No. SKA 178.	Chandler Lake B-4 68°17.580', 152°01.369' East side of Confusion Creek.	Facies 1A Sample from a 35-cm-thick bed of medium-light-gray to medium-gray-weathering, light brownish gray limestone (brachiopod supportstone). Thin section is skeletal-peloidal grainstone (ocally packstone); bioclasts include brachiopod, crinoid, and bryozoan fragments. Sequence 5, HST.	1 incomplete juvenile Pa element *Cavusgnathus* sp. indet. 6 small indet. bar, blade, and platform fragments	late Late Mississippian (Chesterian); age constrained by underlying field No. CC-1.	2.0	Indeterminate; too few conodonts.	Sample from top of the Lisburne Group exposure; shale and spicule unit does not crop out here. Heavy-mineral concentrate contains composite brick-red ferruginous grains, scarce composite fine-grained pyrite, one phosphatized bryozoan fragment, and one ichthyolith. 6.0 kg of rock was processed.

Table 4. Other conodont samples from the study area in northern Alaska.—Continued

[See figures 1 and 2 for locations. All samples collected by J.A. Dumoulin unless otherwise indicated; all faunas identified by A.G. Harris unless otherwise indicated. CAI, conodont color-alteration index; indet., indeterminate; no., number]

Map no., (field, USGS colln. nos.), stratigraphic unit and position	Quadrangle, latitude N., longitude W.	Facies (table 1), lithology, and sequence position	Conodont fauna	Age	CAI	Conodont biofacies and depositional environment	Remarks
			Skimo thrust sheet (cont.)				
Loc. 5, fig. 2 (05AD7A, 34015-PC) Lisburne Group, shale and phosphorite unit; sample from a stratigraphic level close to that of field No. SkBo 20.	Chandler Lake B-5. 68°22.80', 152°50.915' West side of Kiruktagiak River, NW1/4 sec. 28, T. 12 S., R. 4 W.	Facies 5. Sample from a 30- by 8-cm limy concretion in partial section, ~5.7 m thick; phosphorite occurs ~1-2 m above and ~1-2 m below concretion zone. Concretion has weathered surface of concentric yellow-gray and medium-gray rings; fresh surface is medium-dark-gray to black, very fine grained, sooty, and fetid. Thin section is calcareous radiolarite; abundant calcite-replaced radiolarians and lesser calcareous sponge spicules within a matrix of very fine grained carbonate and abundant organic matter. Sequence 5, HST	3 Pa elements *Cavusgnathus regularis* Youngquist and Miller 15 Pa elements (mostly juveniles to subadults) *Gnathodus texanus* Roundy 5 Pa elements *Gnathodus semiglaber* Bischoff [may be redeposited] *Kladognathus tenuis* (Branson and Mehl), emended by Rexroad 1 large Sb and 1 juvenile Sc elements 44 Pa elements *Rhachistognathus prolixus* Baesemann and Lane Unassigned elements: 8 Pb?, 5 M (2 morphotypes), 2 Sa (2 morphotypes), 4 Sb (2 morphotypes), and 6 Sc (3 morphotypes) 497 indet. bar, blade, and very few platform fragments Most conodont blades in this collection have interlamellar organic matter that nicely emphasizes the growth lamellae.	middle Late Mississippian (early Chesterian).	1.0-1.5	Likely deep, anoxic depositional setting (distal winnow?); some larger specimens may have been deposited by way of fecal pellets. Juvenile and subadult forms seem too pristine, delicate, and complete to have undergone turbidite transport. Sample is extremely organic rich and yielded an abundant but relatively low diversity fauna: a chiefly rhachisto-gnathid-gnathodid biofacies.	Sample from section K1 in Kurtak and others (1995). Lisburne Group phosphorite in this area (and at nearby Monotis Creek) is westernmost known occurrence in Chandler Lake quadrangle and is ~40 km northwest of Skimo Creek. Heavy-mineral concentrate is chiefly very fine grained organic matter, with clusters and sprays of barite. 6.0 kg of rock was processed.
Loc. 8, fig. 2 (05PP59C, 33801-PC) Lisburne Group, lime mudstone unit; sample equivalent to field No. SKA 178.	Chandler Lake B-4. 68.31106°, 152.33301° Unnamed central fork of Siksikpuk River; near south-central edge of sec. 15, T. 13 S., R. 2 W.	Facies 1A. Light-brown-gray crinoidal grainstone. Thin section is crinoid-bryozoan grainstone with minor ostracodes, foraminifers, and phosphatic patches. Sequence 5, HST	14 Pa elements *Gnathodus bilineatus* 6 Pa elements *Gnathodus girtyi girtyi* Hass 117 Pa elements *Gnathodus girtyi simplex* Dunn 13 Pa and 1 M elements *Lochriea commutata* (Branson and Mehl) 402 indet. bar, blade, and platform fragments	late Late Mississippian (Chesterian).	1.5-2.0	*Gnathodus girtyi simplex* biofacies; relatively shallow water, relatively high energy, likely normal marine depositional setting (Krumhardt and others, 1996).	Locality is ~17 km west of Skimo Creek. Heavy-mineral concentrate contains abundant weathered pyrite euhedra and euhedral clusters. 5.5 kg of rock was processed. Sample collected by Paige Peapples, Alaska Division of Geological and Geophysical Surveys.

Table 4. Other conodont samples from the study area in northern Alaska.—Continued

[See figures 1 and 2 for locations. All samples collected by J.A. Dumoulin unless otherwise indicated; all faunas identified by A.G. Harris unless otherwise indicated. CAI, conodont color-alteration index; indet., indeterminate; no., number]

Map no., (field, USGS colln. nos.), stratigraphic unit, and position	Quadrangle, latitude N., longitude W.	Facies (table 1), lithology, and sequence position	Conodont fauna	Age	CAI	Conodont biofacies and depositional environment	Remarks
			Skimo thrust sheet (cont.)				
Loc. 17, fig. 2 (04AD11A, 33767-PC) Lisburne Group, top of exposed section; sample likely approximately equivalent to field No. SKA 178.	Chandler Lake B-5 68°19.82', 152°26.84' 0.5 km east of Siksikpuk River; elevation, 3,740 ft; north-central part of sec. 7, T. 13 S., R. 2 W.	Facies 1? Sample from light- to medium-light-gray-weathering, medium- to medium-dark-gray, very fetid limestone (locally partially dolomitized) in 10- to 30-cm-thick irregular beds with bands of brown-gray to black chert (some bands color-laminated, with orange or cream-colored rims). Crinoidal packstone-wackestone, with bryozoans and brachiopods. Thin section is fine-grained skeletal wackestone-packstone with outsized crinoid, brachiopod, and bryozoan fragments (max 4 mm long); smaller bioclasts include algae and ostracodes. Sequence 5. HST	2 large incomplete Pa elements *Cavusgnathus* sp. 1 incomplete Pa *Gnathodus bilineatus* Roundy subsp. indet. 6 Pa *Gnathodus girtyi simplex* Dunn 2 Pa elements *Hindeodus minutus* (Ellison) *Kladognathus* sp. 3 P and 5 Sc element fragments 2 Pa elements *Lochriea commutata* (Branson and Mehl) 14 Pa elements *Rhachistognathus prolixus* Baesemann and Lane 1 Pa *Vogelgnathus postcampbelli* (Austin and Husri) Unassigned elements: 1 Pb and 6 M (at least 3 morphotypes) 172 indet. bar, blade, and platform fragments	late Late Mississippian (Chesterian; no older than upper part of *Gnathodus bilineatus–Upper Cavusgnathus* Zone).	1.5	A very mixed biofacies, best assigned to a rhachistognathid-gnathodid biofacies. Most species are relatively shallow water forms.	Locality is ~ 22 km west of Skimo Creek. Kelley (1988) mapped a small patch of Siksikpuk Formation overlying the Lisburne Group ~2 km east of this locality; regional relations suggest that sample 11A is at or close to the stratigraphic top of the Lisburne Group in this area. Heavy-mineral concentrate contains abundant phosphatic brachiopod fragments, lesser ichthyoliths, and rare dark- to pale-purple and white fluorite. 6.0 kg of rock was processed.
Loc. 17, fig. 2 (04AD11B, 33768-PC) Lisburne Group, just below top of exposed section.	Chandler Lake B-5 68°19.82', 152°26.84'	Facies 1A Sample from light gray-weathering, pale-brownish-gray to pinkish-gray, fetid limestone (crinoidal grainstone) in 10-cm-thick flaggy beds. Thin section is crinoid-bryozoan grainstone with minor muddy patches; other bioclasts include articulated ostracodes, foraminifers, and algae. Sequence 5. HST	13 incomplete Pa elements *Cavusgnathus* sp. indet. 3 Pa element fragments *Gnathodus bilineatus* Roundy 8 incomplete juvenile Pa elements *Gnathodus texanus* Roundy 1 incomplete Pa element *Hindeodus* sp. 1 incomplete M element *Idioprioniodus* sp. indet. 3 Sb-Sc element fragments *Kladognathus* sp. 3 incomplete juvenile Pa elements *Rhachistognathus prolixus* Baesemann and Lane Unassigned elements: 1 Pb, 1 M 230 indet. bar, blade, and platform fragments	middle Late Mississippian (early Chesterian; *Gnathodus bilineatus–Upper Cavusgnathus* Zone).	1.5–2.0	Postmortem transport within or from the cavusgnathid-gnathodid biofacies.	Sample from ~70 cm below sample 11A. Heavy-mineral concentrate includes slightly phosphatic carbonate grains. 6.0 kg of rock was processed.

Table 4. Other conodont samples from the study area in northern Alaska.—Continued

[See figures 1 and 2 for locations. All samples collected by J.A. Dumoulin unless otherwise indicated; all faunas identified by A.G. Harris unless otherwise indicated. CAI, conodont color-alteration index; indet., indeterminate; no., number]

Map no., (field, USGS colln. nos.), stratigraphic unit, and position	Quadrangle, latitude N., longitude W	Facies (table 1), lithology, and sequence position	Conodont fauna	Age	CAI	Conodont biofacies and depositional environment	Remarks
			Skimo thrust sheet (cont.)				
Loc. 20, fig. 2 (TIG-S-190) Lisburne Group, nodular limestone unit; sample from 190 m above base of exposed section and likely approximately equivalent to and thus close to stratigraphic level of field No. SKC 190 (and thus close to stratigraphic level of field No. SKIMO 3).	Chandler Lake B-4 68°17.12', 151°51'48'' South part of Tiglukpuk Creek, SE1/4 sec. 27, T. 13 S., R. 1 E.	Facies 1A? Medium-dark-gray limestone that weathers light gray to faintly blue gray; crinoid supportstone. Thin section is crinoid grainstone with a few muddy patches; other bioclasts include ostracodes, bryozoan fragments, foraminifers, and algae. Many bioclasts are partly to completely replaced by silica; dolomite locally replaces carbonate mud. Sequence 2, HST	3 Pa elements of *Cloghergnathus* sp. transitional to *Cavusgnathus unicornis* Youngquist and Miller 2 Pa cavusgnathid fragments 9 Pa elements *Hindeodus* sp. or *Synclydognathus* sp. 3 indet. elements *Idioprioniodus* sp. indet. *Kladognathus* spp. 3 Pl 13 M, 9 Sb/Sc, and 3 Sa elements 23 Pa elements *Polygnathus communis* Branson and Mehl 1 S element *Synclydognathus geminus* (Hinde) Unassigned elements: 2 Pa, 7 Pb, 1 M, 1 Sc 86 indet. bar, blade, and platform fragments	late Early–early Late Mississippian (very late Osagean–very early Meramecian). *Cloghergnathus* sp. is typical of shallow-water settings with fluctuating, commonly elevated salinities.	2.0	Kladognathid-polygnathid biofacies; relatively shallow water depositional environment.	Locality is ~2 km east of Skimo Creek, from south limb of anticline. Heavy-mineral concentrate contains abundant phosphatized clasts and minor weathered pyrite. 5 kg of rock was processed. Sample collected by Jeff Bever, Petro-Canada Oil & Gas. Collection identified by Andrea Krumhardt, University of Alaska, Fairbanks.
			Thrust sheets south of the Skimo thrust sheet				
Loc. 9, fig. 2 (05AD8C, 34016-PC) Lisburne Group, shale and spiculite unit; likely at or close to stratigraphic level of SKA 187.	Chandler Lake B-4 68°16.905', 152°11.621' Head of small, north-facing gully ~2.1 km due W. of Encampment Creek; SW. cor. sec. 29, T. 13 S., R. 1 W.	Facies 8 Medium-light-gray, glauconitic, skeletal supportstone that weathers grayish orange to pale yellow brown and forms a persistent ~35-cm-thick bed with partings ~10 cm apart. Contains crinoids (max 1 mm diam), black phosphatic grains, and horizontal and oblique burrows (mostly 0.25-0.5 cm diam). Sample from upper 10 cm of bed. Thin section is crinoidal supportstone with fitted fabric, notable glauconite and quartz silt, a few phosphatic grains, and a mud-filled burrow. Bioclasts include bryozoan and brachiopod fragments, foraminifers, ostracodes, and algae(?); some bioclasts are bored. Sequence 6	2 incomplete Pa elements *Gnathodus bilineatus bilineatus* (Roundy) 1 posterior Pa element fragment of *Gnathodus* sp. indet. 1 incomplete Pa *Lochriea commutata* (Branson and Mehl) 1 unassigned Pb element 23 indet. bar, blade, and platform fragments	late Late Mississippian (Chesterian).	1.5-2.0	Normal-marine depositional setting but too few generically identifiable conodonts for biofacies analysis.	Sample from ~11 km west of measured section at Skimo Creek. Glauconitic bed (8C) is overlain by at least 6-8 m of dark lime mudstone. The Siksikpuk Formation is exposed on hill 4002, <1 km to north. Heavy-mineral concentrate contains composite pyrite clusters and single cubes, lesser glauconite-replaced clusters and spines (likely replaced radiolarians), and two large, phosphatized ostracode steinkerns. 6.0 kg of rock was processed.

Table 4. Other conodont samples from the study area in northern Alaska.—Continued

[See figures 1 and 2 for locations. All samples collected by J.A. Dumoulin unless otherwise indicated; all faunas identified by A.G. Harris unless otherwise indicated. CAI, conodont color-alteration index; indet, indeterminate; no, number]

Map no., (field, USGS colln. nos.), stratigraphic unit, and position	Quadrangle, latitude N., longitude W.	Facies (table 1), lithology, and sequence position	Conodont fauna	Age	CAI	Conodont biofacies and depositional environment	Remarks
Thrust sheets south of the Skimo thrust sheet (cont.)							
Loc. 14, fig. 2 (04AD13A, 33769-PC) Lisburne Group. from level likely approximately equivalent to field No. SKA 178.	Chandler Lake A–4 68°11.728', 151°53.967' 2.25 km W. of Soakpak Mountain; elevation, ~5,300 ft; SE1/4 sec. 28, T. 14 S., R. 1 E.	Facies 1A Light- to medium-light-gray-weathering, medium-light-gray, fetid limestone with local bands and nodules of black chert; crinoidal supportstone. Thin section is crinoid-bryozoan grainstone with notable phosphatic grains and patches and minor dolomite and silica replacement; other bioclasts include brachiopod fragments and rare foraminifers. Sequence 5, HST	21 Pa elements *Gnathodus girtyi simplex* Dunn 1 *Idioprioniodus* sp. indet. fragment 2 Pa elements *Lochriea commutata* (Branson and Mehl) 1 Pa element *Rhachistognathus* cf. *Rth. muricatus* 4 Pa elements *Rhachistognathus prolixus* Baesemann and Lane Unassigned elements: 2 Pb (2 morphotypes), 1 M, 130 indet. bar, blade, and platform fragments	late Late Mississippian (upper quarter *Gnathodus bilineatus*-Upper *Cavusgnathus* Zone to top of Chesterian).	1.5–2.0	Postmortem transport within or from a rhachistognathid-gnathodid biofacies.	Sample from 5-cm-thick bed at top of massive cliff of the Lisburne Group that underlies rubble of gray- to brown-weathering, dark-gray to black silty to limy mudstone which likely correlates with the shale and spiculite unit at Skimo Creek. Above this rubble is an outcrop. 40 cm thick, of gray glauconitic limestone that is the top of the Lisburne here; it is immediately overlain by gray siltstone of the Siksikpuk Formation. Heavy-mineral concentrate is chiefly phosphatic grains (including ichthyoliths, pelmatozoan ossicles, phosphatic brachiopod fragments, and other phosphatic and phosphatized grains) with scarce composite pyrite grains. 6.0 kg of rock was processed.
Loc. 15, fig. 2 (AKA 16-1, 29606-PC) Uppermost part of the Lisburne Group at this locality.	Chandler Lake A–4 68°12.25', 151°51.35' Soakpak Mountain, sec. 26, T. 14 S., R. 1 E.	Light-brown-weathering, light-gray limestone (crinoidal-bryozoan grainstone) directly beneath the Siksikpuk Formation; contact is sharp and undulatory. Upper part of bed contains glauconite, phosphatic clasts, and nodular and disseminated pyrite. Thin section is crinoidal grainstone with notable glauconite, phosphatic clasts, a large phosphatic nodule, minor quartz silt, and disseminated pyrite. Other bioclasts include bryozoan and ostracode fragments; some bioclasts are bored and (or) partially phosphatized.	1 slightly incomplete Pa element *Adetognathus lautus* (Gunnell) 1 waterworm Pa element *Gnathodus girtyi simplex* Dunn transitional to *Gn. defectus* Dunn 1 waterworm posterior platform element *Gn. defectus* Dunn? 1 incomplete Pa element *Gnathodus* cf. *Gn. bilineatus* Roundy 1 incomplete element *Rhachistognathus primus* Dunn 2 posterior element fragments *Rhachistognathus* sp. indet. 1 unassigned incomplete Sa element 17 indet. bar, blade, and platform fragments	Latest Mississippian-earliest Pennsylvanian (very late Chesterian-very earliest Morrowan; *Rhachistognathus primus* Zone into lowermost *Declinognathodus noduliferus* Zone)	2.5–3.0	Indeterminate; too few conodonts. Fauna is a postmortem mixture of shallow-water, likely high energy (shoal) species.	Soakpak Mountain section of Adams (1991, 1994); age of this collection originally reported as Pennsylvanian (early Morrowan), based on examination by Harris in 1985 (USGS fossil report O-85-21). Collection reexamined and age revised by Harris in 2004. Heavy-mineral concentrate contained one ichthyolith, one phosphatized bryozoan steinkern, one bryozoan fragment, and one spine. Sample collected by Karen Adams, University of Alaska, Fairbanks.

Table 4. Other conodont samples from the study area in northern Alaska.—Continued

[See figures 1 and 2 for locations. All samples collected by J.A. Dumoulin unless otherwise indicated; all faunas identified by A.G. Harris unless otherwise indicated. CAI, conodont color-alteration index; indet., indeterminate; no., number]

Map no., (field, USGS colln. nos.), stratigraphic unit, and position	Quadrangle, latitude N., longitude W.	Facies (table 1), lithology, and sequence position	Conodont fauna	Age	CAI	Conodont biofacies and depositional environment	Remarks
			Thrust sheets south of the Skimo thrust sheet (cont.)				
Loc. 16, fig. 2 (04AD14, 33770-PC) Kayak Shale	Chandler Lake A-4 68°12.432', 151°53.442' 2.7 km NW. of Soakpak Mountain; elevation, 5,320 ft; SE corner sec. 21, T. 14 S., R. 1 E.	Facies not determined. Pale-yellow-orange- to moderate-yellow-brown-weathering, medium-dark-gray to dark-gray lime mudstone with rare crinoids and possible colonial coral. Thin section is overpacked skeletal packstone with minor dolomitic and quartz silt; bioclasts include coral, bryozoan, crinoid, and brachiopod fragments, gastropods, ostracodes, and calcareous sponge spicules. Sequence 1?	3 juvenile Pa elements *Polygnathus communis* Branson and Mehl; 6 Pa elements *Polygnathus inornatus* E.R. Branson; 6 Pa element fragments *Polygnathus* spp.; 2 Pa element fragments *Pseudopolygnathus*? sp. indet.; 1 Pa element *Bispathodus aculeatus* Branson and Mehl; 2 M elements of Mississippian morphotype and 2 Sc elements; 19 indet. bar and blade fragments	early Early Mississippian (Kinderhookian)	2.0–2.5	Postmortem transport within and (or) from a polygnathid biofacies.	Heavy-mineral concentrate is chiefly phosphatic bioclasts and partly phosphatic composite carbonate grains; in order of decreasing abundance, bioclasts are ichthyoliths, smooth-shelled ostracode steinkerns, and phosphatic brachiopod fragments. 6.0 kg of rock was processed.
Loc. 18, fig. 2 (SOAK-TOP, 33749-PC) Lisburne Group; from stratigraphic level possibly equivalent to that of field No. SKA 187.	Chandler Lake A-3 68°13', 151°40' (location approximate)	Facies 1A? Medium-gray limestone that weathers very pale yellowish brown; fine-grained bryozoan supportstone. Thin section is pelmatozoan-bryozoan grainstone with notable phosphatic clasts and bioclasts and minor detrital quartz silt. Sequence 6?	2 Pa element fragments *Gnathodus bilineatus* Roundy or *Gn. bollandensis* (though abraded and incomplete, these are more like *Gn. bollandensis*); 28 Pa elements *Gnathodus defectus* Dunn; 6 Pa elements *Gnathodus girtyi simplex* Dunn; 21 *Idioprioniodus* sp. indet. element fragments; 3 Pa elements *Lochriea commutata* (Branson and Mehl); 35 Pa elements *Rhachistognathus primus* Dunn; 4 Pa elements *Rhachistognathus prolixus* Baesemann and Lane; 2 Pa elements *Rhachistognathus websteri* Baesemann and Lane; 20 Pa element fragments *Rhachistognathus* spp. indet.; 147 indet. bar, blade, and platform fragments	Very late Late Mississippian (very late Chesterian); *Gnathodus girtyi* subspp. and *Lochriea commutata* are restricted to the Chesterian and *Gn. bilineatus* extends into the late Meramecian, but *Idioprioniodus* sp. and all the rhachistognathid species cross the mid-Carboniferous boundary. Species association thus indicates a very late Chesterian age.	2.5–3.0	Rhachistognathid-gnathodid biofacies. The collection is a lag concentrate because no juvenile platform elements and virtually all the more delicate and lighter ramiform elements are missing, indicating postmortem hydraulic sorting. The abundance of rhachistognathids indicates a nearby high-energy shoal-water facies.	Northwest of Soakpak Mountain on the west side of the Anaktuvuk River valley, just under klippe of the Lisburne Group and close to contact with the overlying Siksikpuk Formation as mapped by Kelley (1988). Sample from stratigraphically highest Lisburne outcrop, overlain by covered slope that may be equivalent to the shale and spiculite unit at Skimo Creek. Heavy-mineral concentrate consists chiefly of phosphatic brachiopod fragments with lesser phosphatized rock fragments and crinoid ossicles. 6.4 kg of rock was processed. Sample collected by geologists from Petro-Canada Oil & Gas.

Table 4. Other conodont samples from the study area in northern Alaska.—Continued

[See figures 1 and 2 for locations. All samples collected by J.A. Dumoulin unless otherwise indicated; all faunas identified by A.G. Harris unless otherwise indicated. CAI, conodont color-alteration index; indet., indeterminate; no., number]

Map no., (field, USGS colln. nos.), stratigraphic unit, and position	Quadrangle, latitude N., longitude W.	Facies (table 1), lithology, and sequence position	Conodont fauna	Age	CAI	Conodont biofacies and depositional environment	Remarks
			Tiglukpuk thrust sheet				
Loc. 11, fig. 2 (05AD21, 34(14-PC) Lisburne Group. chert and phosphorite unit: sample likely approximately equivalent to field No. TNC 190.	Chandler Lake B-4 68°22.595′, 151°57.078′ Saddle SE. of peak 3874. ~0.4 km W. of main fork of Tiglukpuk Creek, NW1/4 sec. 29, T. 12 S., R. 1 E.,	Facies 1A Light-gray-weathering, dark brownish-gray limestone with local silicified brachiopods in beds as much as 20 cm thick; appears to underlie phosphate zone, west end of the Tiglupuk anticline. Thin section is fine-grained peloidal-skeletal grainstone. Bioclasts include brachiopod and crinoid fragments, calcispheres, algae, and foraminifers; many bioclasts are broken, and some may be micritized. Sequence 5 (TST?)	14 juvenile Pa elements *Bispathodus utahensis* Sandberg and Gutschick 2 adult Pa elements *Cavusgnathus regularis* Youngquist and Miller 7 juvenile Pa elements *Cavusgnathus unicornis* Youngquist and Miller 10 incomplete Pa elements *Cavusgnathus* spp.(?) indet. 30 Pa elements *Gnathodus texanus* Roundy 11 juvenile Pa elements *Gnathodus* sp. (likely *Gn. texanus* Roundy) *Kladognathus tenuis* (Branson and Mehl), emended by Rexroad 3 bar fragments and 2 Sa, 2 incomplete Sb, and 2 Sc elements Unassigned elements: 19 Pb (2 morphotypes), 9 M (2 morphotypes), 3 Sa (2 morphotypes), and 20 Sc (3 morphotypes) 676 indet. bar, blade, and platform fragments	middle Late Mississippian (early Chesterian, likely no younger than *Gnathodus bilineatus*–Upper *Cavusgnathus* Zone).	1.5–2.0	Distal winnow of mixed biofacies.	Sample on trend with and 3.2 km west of the Tiglukpuk anticline measured section (TNA-TND). Heavy-mineral concentrate consists overwhelmingly of conodonts (mostly juveniles, small fragments, and scarce complete elements) but also contains rare pyrite and glauconite. 6.0 kg of rock was processed.

Table 4.   Other conodont samples from the study area in northern Alaska.—Continued

[See figures 1 and 2 for locations. All samples collected by J.A. Dumoulin unless otherwise indicated; all faunas identified by A.G. Harris unless otherwise indicated. CAI, conodont color-alteration index; indet., indeterminate; no, number]

Map no., (field, USGS colln. nos.), stratigraphic unit, and position	Quadrangle, latitude N., longitude W.	Facies (table 1), lithology, and sequence position	Conodont fauna	Age	CAI	Conodont biofacies and depositional environment	Remarks
			Tiglukpuk thrust sheet (cont.)				
Loc. 13, fig. 2 (05AD9C, 34017-PC). Lisburne Group, upper packstone and grainstone unit; sample from highest supportstone bed, which should be close to the stratigraphic level of field No. TND 55.	Chandler Lake B-4 68°22.592´, 152°06.565´ West-facing bluff, east side of Encampment Creek; elevation, ~2,360 ft; NW1/4 sec. 27, T. 12 S., R. 1 W.	Facies 1 Light-brown-gray-weathering, very light gray to medium-light-gray crinoidal supportstone; very fetid, contains dead oil, and may be in part dolomitic. Sample from bed ~1.25 m thick. Thin section is overpacked crinoid-bryozoan grainstone with minor muddy patches and numerous stylolites. Sequence 5, HST	4 nearly complete Pa elements *Cavusgnathus regularis* Youngquist and Miller 30 large incomplete Pa elements *Cavusgnathus* sp. 7 nearly complete Pa elements *Gnathodus bollandensis* (Higgins and Bouckaert) 22 incomplete juvenile and adult Pa elements *Gnathodus bilineatus* (Roundy) and (or) *Gn. bilineatus bollandensis* (Higgins and Bouckaert) 5 incomplete Pa elements *Gnathodus* cf. *Gn. girtyi* Hass 13 Pa *Gnathodus girtyi simplex* Dunn 5 juvenile Pa elements *Gnathodus* cf. *Gn. girtyi simplex* Dunn 16 mainly incomplete Pa elements *Gnathodus texanus* Roundy 2 Pa elements *Hindeodus minutus* (Ellison) *Kladognathus tenuis* (Branson and Mehl), emended by Rexroad 3 P, 4 Sb-Sc, and 6 Sc fragments 2 Pa elements *Lochriea commutata* (Branson and Mehl) 1 Pa *Vogelgnathus postcampbelli* (Austin and Husri) Unassigned elements: 4 Pb (3 morphotyes), 9 M (at least 4 morphotypes), and 1 Sc 664 indet. bar, blade, and platform fragments	middle Mississippian (early Chesterian, likely no younger than *Gn. bilineatus*-Upper *Cavusgnathus* Zone).	1.5–2.0	Mixed biofacies: heavy-mineral concentrate consists of a relatively diverse species association of mainly incomplete conodont elements dominated by gnathodids and cavusgnathids with rare shallower water species of *Vogelgnathus* and *Hindeodus*.	Sample from same thrust sheet as, but ~10 km west of, Tiglukpuk Creek section. Supportstone sampled as 9C overlain by ~10-15 m of light-weathering lime mudstone and then ~25-30 m of dark-weathering lime mudstone, shale, and glauconitic siltstone. Heavy-mineral concentrate consists chiefly of conodonts (mostly fragments). 6.0 kg of rock was processed.

Table 4. Other conodont samples from the study area in northern Alaska.—Continued

[See figures 1 and 2 for locations. All samples collected by J.A. Dumoulin unless otherwise indicated; all faunas identified by A.G. Harris unless otherwise indicated. CAI, conodont color-alteration index; indet., indeterminate; no., number]

Map no., (field, USGS colln. nos.), stratigraphic unit, and position	Quadrangle, latitude N., longitude W.	Facies (table 1), lithology, and sequence position	Conodont fauna	Age	CAI	Conodont biofacies and depositional environment	Remarks
				Tiglukpuk thrust sheet (cont.)			
Loc. 13, fig. 2 (05AD91, 34018-PC) Lisburne Group, shale and lime mudstone unit, stratigraphically higher than any conodont sample from the Tiglukpuk Creek section and likely equivalent to field No. SKA 187.	Chandler Lake B-4 68°22.592′, 152°06.565′ West-facing bluff, east side of Encampment Creek; elevation ~2,360 ft	Facies 8 Sample from irregular beds (3 cm thick) of medium-gray to brownish-black, fine-grained glauconitic limestone that weathers pale yellow-brown and contains black phosphatic grains, rare gastropods, and horizontal and oblique trace fossils. Thin section is muddy calcareous siltstone with notable glauconitic and pyrite, a few phosphatic clasts and nodules, and minor quartz silt; rare bioclasts are mainly crinoid fragments. Sequence 6	4 mid-Pa element fragments of *Bispathodus utahensis* Sandberg and Gutschick 1 Pa element *Gnathodus* sp., possibly *Gn. girtyi* Hass 1 Pa element fragment *Gnathodus* sp., possibly fragment of *Gn. bilineatus* (Roundy) 138 indet. bar, blade, and platform fragments	middle Late Mississippian (early Chesterian).	1.5–2.0	Too few generically identifiable conodonts for biofacies analysis. Conodonts likely transported from normal marine depositional setting.	Sample from ~0.5 m above base of interval ~25–30 m thick of dark-weathering lime mudstone, shale, and glauconitic siltstone. Heavy-mineral concentrate contains abundant partly pyritic and carbonaceous carbonate grains. 6.0 kg of rock was processed.
				Structural position uncertain			
Loc. 19, fig. 2 (PP-03-027) Lisburne Group, sample from ~3–4 m below highest exposed part of the Lisburne Group, and ~5 m below basal Siksikpuk Formation.	Chandler Lake B-2 68.35920°, 150.79439° 2 km east of Erratic Creek, east-central part of sec. 31, T. 12 S., R. 6 E.	Facies 1 Upper part of the Lisburne Group. Light-gray, slightly dolomitic(?) limestone that weathers grayish orange to medium light gray. Abundant crinoid ossicles; fractures coated with black (organic?) material. Thin section is overpacked crinoidal supportstone with subordinate bryozoan and phosphatic skeletal fragments and minor glauconite. Sequence 6?	77 Pa elements *Gnathodus girtyi girtyi* Hass 172 Pa elements *Gnathodus girtyi simplex* Dunn 63 Pa elements *Gnathodus girtyi girtyi* spp. indet 4 Pa elements *Gnathodus girtyi simplex* Dunn transitional to *Declinognathodus noduliferus japonicus* (Igo and Koike) 6 Pa elements *Hindeodus*? spp. indet *Idioprioniodus* spp. indet. 5 Pb?, 4 M?, 29 Sc?* elements *Kladognathus*? spp. indet. 1 Sb-Sc, 1 Sa elements 23 Pa elements *Rhachistognathus muricatus* (Dunn) 62 Pa elements *Rhachistognathus prolixus* Baesmann and Lane 19 Pa elements *Vogelgnathus campbelli* (Rexroad) 23 Pa elements *Vogelgnathus postcampbelli* (Austin and Husri) Unassigned elements: 70 Pa, 2 Pb, 1M, 1Sc 63 indet. bar, blade, and platform fragments	Latest Mississippian (late, likely very late, Chesterian).	2.0–3.0	Gnathodid-rhachistognathid biofacies; normal marine, above wave base.	Sample from ~10 km east of Shainin Lake. Structural position of this sample relative to the Skimo and Tiglukpuk thrust sheets is uncertain. Heavy-mineral concentrate is chiefly weathered pyrite. 13.7 kg of rock processed. 5 trays picked for all elements, rest picked for identifiable morphotypes. Sample collected by Paige Peapples, Alaska Division of Geological and Geophysical Surveys. Collection identified by Andrea Krumhardt, University of Alaska, Fairbanks.

Table 4. Other conodont samples from the study area in northern Alaska.—Continued

[See figures 1 and 2 for locations. All samples collected by J.A. Dumoulin unless otherwise indicated; all faunas identified by A.G. Harris unless otherwise indicated. CAI, conodont color-alteration index; indet., indeterminate; no., number]

Map no., (field, USGS colln. nos.), stratigraphic unit, and position	Quadrangle, latitude N., longitude W.	Facies (table 1), lithology, and sequence position	Conodont fauna	Age	CAI	Conodont biofacies and depositional environment	Remarks
Structural position uncertain (cont.)							
Loc. 21, fig. 2 (04BS6A, 33782-PC) Clast of Lisburne Group(?) in debris-flow unit of Okpikruak Formation.	Chandler Lake B-4 68°20'40"; 151°52'07"	Yellow-gray-weathering, pinkish-gray limestone; crinoidal packstone-grainstone with bryozoan fragments. Sample is about two-thirds of a clast that was several tens of centimeters long. Thin section is partially dolomitized crinoidal packstone with one large brachiopod shell fragment (0.5 cm diam).	6 Pa element fragments *Cavusgnathus* sp. indet. and (or) *Adetognathus* sp. indet. 1 unassigned M element fragment 2 Sc element fragments *Kladognathus* sp. indet. 23 partly waterworn indet. bar, blade, and platform fragments	Late Mississippian (late Meramecian-Chesterian).	2.5	Indeterminate (too few identifiable conodonts); conodont species association and their taphonomy indicate derivation from a shallow-water, high-energy depositional setting.	Sample obtained to test age, affinity, and CAI of probable Lisburne Group clast; was clast derived from the Endicott Mountains allochthon or from a higher-level allochthon? Lithofacies and biofacies of this sample were not distinctive enough to be certain. Heavy-mineral concentrate contains minor phosphatic and phosphatized bioclasts (ichthyoliths and rare bryozoan fragments), and rare very pale purple to clear fluorite. 6.0 kg of rock was processed.

www.ingramcontent.com/pod-product-compliance
Lightning Source LLC
Chambersburg PA
CBHW080437290526
45791CB00008BA/2534